The Guy's GUIDE

TO GOD, GIRLS,

AND THE PHONE IN YOUR POCKET

{ 101 REAL-WORLD TIPS FOR TEENAGE GUYS }

JONATHAN McKEE

SHILOH RUN

Print ISBN 978-1-62416-990-8

eBook Editions:
Adobe Digital Edition (.epub) 978-1-63058-047-6
Kindle and MobiPocket Edition (.prc) 978-1-63058-048-3

Cover Design: Greg Jackson, Thinkpen Design

The author is represented by, and this book is published in association with, the literary agency of WordServe Literary Group, Ltd., www.wordserveliterary.com.

Published by Shiloh Run Press, an imprint of Barbour Publishing, Inc., P.O. Box 719, Uhrichsville, Ohio 44683
www.shilohrunpress.com

Our mission is to publish and distribute inspirational products offering exceptional value and biblical encouragement to the masses.

Member of the
Evangelical Christian
Publishers Association

Printed in the United States of America.

DEDICATED TO A BRILLIANT
YOUNG BOY NAMED AIDAN,
CLINGING TO THE TRUTH
IN A WORLD FULL OF LIES.

ACKNOWLEDGMENTS

WHEN THIS BOOK WAS STILL IN THE PROPOSAL STAGE, I asked countless family members and friends, "What advice would you give to today's teenage guys?" Many of these tips came from those conversations.

I have to especially thank my own three teenagers, Alec, Alyssa, and Ashley, for sharing a number of great ideas, as well as their candid thoughts about what teenagers experience today.

I can't thank my wife, Lori, enough, not only for the wisdom she shared on many of these pages, but also for putting up with me during the writing process. She can attest to numerous nights lying awake in bed talking about this book (when she probably would have preferred sleep).

Thanks to my good friend Scott Allgier for sitting under that canopy by the lake with a Bible and a computer, dialoguing about this book and discussing at length the advice we'd like our own teen sons to glean. Scott endured numerous texts like this one: PICTURE WE'RE UNDER THE CANOPY AGAIN, AND NOW I'M LOOKING FOR A SCRIPTURE ABOUT. . .

Scott is an amazing man of God and discipler of men.

Thanks to my friend David R. Smith for many of these tips. David doesn't just come up with good discipleship advice, he lives it with his own son, Josiah, and several young men he has discipled into ministry.

Thanks to all my blog readers at JonathanMcKeeWrites.com who came in with some great advice when I blogged about the subject. Many of these tips are composite versions of your advice. Thanks for being loyal readers!

Special thanks to Kelly McIntosh at Barbour for truly working with me to keep this book real and relevant to teenage guys. I was surprised by how open she was to keeping this project brutally honest and—dare I say—*explicit*, when needed. You're a team player, Kelly! I won't forget that.

Thanks most of all to God for His grace and mercy in my life. I'm so imperfect, it's obvious that any good wisdom in this book comes from Him, not me.

CONTENTS

After receiving the Ultimate Choice Award at the 2013 Teen Choice Awards, actor Ashton Kutcher did something unusual during his acceptance speech. He used the opportunity to share some advice.

"Okay, let's be brutally honest. . . " he said.

And that's what he was. He began by sharing that Ashton wasn't even his real first name. His first name is actually Chris. Ashton is his middle name. Then he went on to reveal the three most important things he learned when he was still known as Chris: work hard; be smart, thoughtful, and generous; and build a life for yourself.

The most interesting element of his speech was the crowd's reaction. Most of the young people in the audience didn't know how to respond. Some cheered awkwardly at random moments; some were silent. They weren't used to hearing this kind of sincere advice from one of their role models.

For the next week, the media talked about Ashton Kutcher's four-minute speech more than any other element of the show, with headlines like FAMOUS ACTOR GIVES INCREDIBLY INSIGHTFUL SPEECH. Apparently, people were shocked to hear something positive coming from that stage.

Where are young people gleaning advice today?

When this book was still in the proposal stage, I sent my family a group text and asked, WHAT ADVICE WOULD YOU GIVE TODAY'S TEENAGE GUYS?

My phone started blowing up with group replies—more than twenty texts in the next five minutes. All really good stuff.

From my son: LISTEN MORE THAN YOU SPEAK.

From my elder daughter: ALWAYS MAKE SURE YOU SMELL GOOD. GUYS DON'T REALIZE HOW IMPORTANT IT IS TO GIRLS.

Then I blogged about it and asked my readers. A hundred more pieces of advice poured in.

LUST IS NEVER SATISFIED.

YOU'RE NOT TRYING TO BECOME A BIG BOY; YOU'RE TRYING TO BECOME A MAN.

YOUR XBOX GAMERSCORE WILL NOT APPEAR ON YOUR RÉSUMÉ. PUT YOUR CONTROLLER DOWN EVERY ONCE IN A WHILE AND GO OUTSIDE!

As I began going through the answers, I noticed a common denominator. The answers were all candid, straightforward—even blunt. It was as if people felt this advice was typically shouted into deaf ears.

Is it that young men today don't want to hear advice, or is good advice just rare?

As I embarked on the journey of writing this book, taking everything to heart, I refused to consider what would sell or market well; instead, I wrote the explicit truth that teenage guys need to hear.

In the words of Chris Ashton Kutcher, "Okay, let's be brutally honest. . . ."

REALIZE THAT MOST BAD DECISIONS BEGAN FIVE CHOICES AGO.

STOP FLIRTING WITH DISASTER.

It usually starts with something small: a small lie, a seemingly insignificant decision to go to a friend's house when his parents aren't home, or a click on a website that is known to have inappropriate content. It doesn't seem like a big deal at the time, but with each choice, we take one step closer to temptation.

The small lie works, but a few days later you're questioned about it, and you cover it up with a bigger lie. That lie gives birth to others, and before you know it, you're waist deep in deception and you're wondering how you got there.

It all started five choices ago, with a small lie.

Your friend texts you and invites you to his house on Friday night, even though his parents won't be home. *No big deal,* you tell yourself. When you arrive, your friends are drinking. You don't want to be snobby and leave, so you decide to just "hang" and hope they don't offer you anything. Before long, your friend pours you a drink. You don't want to make a scene, so you thank him and just hold the glass. It doesn't work. Within five minutes your friend notices and asks you point-blank, "Aren't you gonna try it?" Everyone is staring at you. How do you say no? It's so difficult when you're in that situation!

Was it as difficult five choices ago when you first received the text?

You're working on some homework and you take your laptop computer into your bedroom and close the door. After an hour of homework, you take a break and check your friends' status on your favorite sites. You see a link that reads "hilarious," but it has a picture of a girl in some revealing clothes. It's not nudity, so you click on the site and watch the video. Sure enough, it is really funny. . .and a little bit racy. Now you're thinking about the girl in the video. The site provides plenty of links, including one that is sure to take you to more videos with girls like the one you just saw. A few links later, you're looking at full nudity. You don't even know how you got there. . .but it seemed nearly impossible to stop or turn back.

Was it impossible to resist when you decided to take your computer into your room and shut the door?

Small choices open doors to bigger decisions. We may think it's no big deal to tell a little fib or go to a friend's house when his parents are gone or go behind closed doors with a computer. But often we're just fooling ourselves and inviting temptation.

Stop flirting with disaster.

Don't get me wrong. It's impossible to avoid every temptation in life. We can't hide ourselves in the basement and never go outside. (Don't try it; it's not fun.) Temptations will always surface. But when you run across something tempting, steer clear of it. Don't walk toward it. The closer you get, the more you're playing with fire.

The apostle Paul gives us some good advice:

> *No temptation has overtaken you except what is common to mankind. And God is faithful; he will not let you be tempted beyond what you can bear. But when you are tempted, he will also provide a way out so that you can endure it.* (1 Corinthians 10:13 NIV)

That's just it; God always provides a way of escape. But let's be honest: sometimes, instead of looking for a way to escape, we try to see how close we can get to the temptation without giving in. Then we wonder, *Why was that so difficult to resist?*

We probably should have fixed our eyes on the escape route five choices ago!

GO AHEAD, ANSWER. . .

+ In the examples above, what were some ways of early escape?

+ Why don't people use these escape routes while it's still easy?

+ What are some situations where you have seen small decisions lead to bigger choices?

+ What escape routes could you have taken?

+ Why didn't you?

FINAL THOUGHTS

As we spend time getting to know God and trusting Him in everyday decisions, we'll begin to rely on Him to help us look for escape routes early. Don't flirt with danger. Look for the ways out that God provides.

TURN OFF YOUR SMARTPHONE BEFORE YOU CRAWL INTO BED.

WHEN IT'S BEDTIME, PUT YOUR IPHONE TO BED AS WELL. Give it a good-night kiss on the screen if you'd like, but then put it away. You don't need it on during the night.

Start a new habit if you must. As you brush your teeth, post your status one last time and then power down for the night. Your friends don't need to be able to get ahold of you. You don't need to be "connected" during the wee hours of the night. Human beings have been sleeping without technology for thousands of years. You can swing it.

Researchers have discovered that teenagers need anywhere from 8.5 to 9.25 hours of sleep per night to recharge mentally and physically for the next day. Most teens, however, average 6.5 to 7.5 hours of sleep per night due to self-imposed demanding schedules, too much caffeine, and. . .yes. . .an overin-dulgence of technology.[1] In other words, a busy schedule, a can of Red Bull, and your smartphone are costing you a good night's sleep!

These research findings are pretty scary. The physical consequences of a lack of sleep include diabetes, depression, decreased self-control, and falling asleep at the wheel. (Drowsy driving causes more than 100,000 accidents and 1,500 deaths a year.) Lack of sleep also affects brain circuitry and hormone regulation.

Our brains need rest. According to the experts, students usually have a better chance of doing well on a test if they've gotten a good night's sleep, rather than sacrificing sleep to cram in some last-minute studying. (Of course, if the student had simply put down the game controller after school and studied then, he would have been ready for the test *and* gotten enough sleep!)

So how do our smartphones contribute to our lack of sleep?

1. The phones wake us up after we've fallen asleep. Even if we go to bed on time, our friends may not be on the same schedule. In the most recent Sleep in America poll, almost 1 in 5 teens admitted to being woken up one or more times per night from a text and sometimes even a call.[2]

2. Our phones keep us from relaxing and unwinding. Let's face it: today's phones are much more than just phones. They are technological Swiss Army knives—a phone, computer, calendar, GPS, YouTube, Google, games, camera. . .the list goes on. Many of these activities get us wired or amped up so we can't go to sleep. Games can boost adrenaline, and bright screens can actually suppress the secretion of melatonin, the hormone that induces sleepiness. On top of all that, a text from Chris informing us what Ashley said might make us mad! It's impossible to sleep when our hearts are racing.

I know. It's not fun to have to turn off such a cool gadget. But it's also not fun flunking a math quiz, getting suspended for losing your cool and fighting, or falling asleep on the drive home, all because you felt the need to stay up half the night texting Chris and Amanda about what a pain Ashley is!

GO AHEAD, ANSWER. . .

+ What are some of your favorite features or apps on your phone?

+ How might these become a distraction to you, day or night?

+ Do you keep your phone on at night? If so, how often does it disturb your sleep? Be honest.

+ How is your phone most likely to wake you at night?

+ Given what all the doctors and other experts recommend, what do you think is the wise thing to do?

+ How can you start this habit this week?

FINAL THOUGHTS

Your sleep is more important than Ashley. (Who is this Ashley anyway? Do we need to have a talk?. . .) Turn off your phone at night. The consequences of leaving it on are pretty straightforward, and let's be real: you aren't going to miss much if it's off. Do yourself a favor and power down when you brush your teeth.

TELL YOUR PARENTS TO BLOCK THAT CHANNEL.
(YOU KNOW THE ONE I'M TALKING ABOUT.)

TECHNOLOGY SENDS IMAGES TO YOUR HOUSE THROUGH numerous portals, but none is as vivid, large, and hi-def as those flowing into your television screen.

When I say TV, I'm not just talking about *The Cosby Show* anymore. (That's a show your parents watched when they were younger.) I'm talking about the shows that *show* way too much. You know the ones I'm talking about.

When I was a kid, we had four channels: NBC, CBS, ABC, and PBS. If you had a special antenna, you could also get FOX. TV was free back then. Few people paid for cable, and satellite was nonexistent.

Fast forward to now. Ninety-one percent of American homes pay for TV.[3] People have as many as nine hundred channels, including premium channels and pay-per-view just a click away.

This introduces a lot of distractions into our homes. Yes, even if our parents don't subscribe to premium channels, shows like *Two and a Half Men* and *Family Guy* provide us with the sex education we didn't get from our parents.

But what about those channels that show us even more?

Maybe Mom and Dad don't realize some of the temptations we experience on our television screens.

GO AHEAD, ANSWER. . .

Ask yourself these candid (and potentially embarrassing) questions:

+ In the last few months, have you watched something on one of your screens that would have embarrassed you if one of your parents had walked in?

+ In the last few months, have you watched something your parents don't want you watching?

+ In the last few months, have you ever found yourself lusting while looking at an image on a screen?

+ In the last few months, have you masturbated while looking at a screen? (It's an embarrassing question, but you're just answering it to yourself anyway.)

+ Do you know a password that allows you to see something you're not supposed to see?

+ Are you tempted by the content on a premium channel (HBO, Showtime, etc.)?

Did you answer yes to any of these questions?

In this book we'll look at several passages about lust (Matthew 5:27–30) and fleeing sexual temptation (1 Corinthians 6:18). Let's look at yet another piece of good advice, from 2 Timothy 2:22:

> *Run from anything that stimulates youthful lusts. Instead, pursue righteous living, faithfulness, love, and peace. Enjoy the companionship of those who call on the Lord with pure hearts.*

+ According to the verse, what should we run from?
+ What are some examples of "youthful lusts" in your life?
+ How can you "run" from these?
+ Whom can you ask to help you with this?

It's great to have friends and a mentor with whom you can talk, pray, and discuss temptations candidly. I recommend you have people like that in your life. But I also encourage you to take the very bold step of letting your parents know if they need to block a channel or make use of a new password, removing a temptation from your life.

Yes, this could be embarrassing, and it might even provoke a discussion you're not sure you want to have. But most parents will respect their kids for being honest enough to tell them the truth.

FINAL THOUGHTS

Do you have a temptation in your house that needs to be removed? Don't hesitate. Go to your parents now and simply say. . .

"Dad, I need you to get rid of that TV in my room."
"Mom, I need you to get a new password."
"Dad, I need you to cancel HBO."
You'll be glad you did.

TODAY'S NERD IS TOMORROW'S BOSS.

IT HAPPENS CONSISTENTLY, AND ALWAYS IN PE CLASS.
The bullies begin roaming in search of the perfect nerd to slap on the back of the legs, shove into a garbage can, or hang on a locker hook by his underwear. If only those bullies knew they were torturing *their future boss*!

Have you ever seen a picture of Microsoft's Bill Gates, now one of the richest men in the world?

Total nerd! *A total nerd driving a half-million-dollar Porsche 959!*

How about Mark Zuckerberg, creator of Facebook?

Big-time nerd!

So, if you're a bully, think twice about who you're giving a wedgie. You might be turning in an application to his company someday.

And if you're a nerd who actually studies and works hard while the bullies are sitting on their behinds? Don't worry. The tables will turn. Your hard work will pay off.

Proverbs 10:4 says it about as simply as it can be said:

> *Lazy hands make for poverty, but diligent hands bring wealth.* (NIV)

GO AHEAD, ANSWER. . .

+ According to Proverbs 10:4, what is the result of lazy hands?

+ Do you think this is true? Explain.

+ What does *diligent* mean?

+ What do diligent hands bring?

+ Can you give an example of this?

+ Why do bullies bully?

+ Describe a time when you were bullied (if any).

+ Describe a time you might have used your size or position in an intimidating manner.

+ What would you like to be known for?

FINAL THOUGHTS

People who work hard usually are rewarded for their labor. It might not seem like it during middle school PE class. . . but just give it a few years. Today's nerd is tomorrow's boss.

CHOOSE YOUR FRIENDS WISELY, BECAUSE THE PEOPLE YOU SURROUND YOURSELF WITH REFLECT WHO YOU ARE.

BE CAREFUL WHO YOU SURROUND YOURSELF WITH. DON'T take it from me. Take it from actor Will Smith: "The best thing that anybody ever said to me is that you're only as good as the people you associate with. Look at the five friends that you spend the most time with—that's who you are."[4]

GO AHEAD, ANSWER. . .

+ Is Will Smith right? Explain.

+ Explain how a guy's five closest friends could slowly change him.

+ Do you think most people would admit this is the case? Why?

+ What are some good traits you have absorbed from your friends?

+ What are some bad habits you might be gleaning from your friends?

+ Why do you think Will Smith calls this the best advice anybody ever gave him?

+ Name someone you should spend more time with.

+ How can you initiate that this week?

Most people are far more influenced by their friends than they realize. If our friends make bad choices, it's very difficult to hang out with them and make good choices for ourselves. Conversely, if our friends are always making good choices, it's hard to make bad choices around them.

Proverbs 22:24–25 gives us a peek at the power of the people we surround ourselves with:

> Don't befriend angry people or associate with hot-tempered people, or you will learn to be like them and endanger your soul.

These verses say it plainly. Hang out with a bad influence, and you'll learn to be like that person. Worse yet, hanging out with bad influences will endanger your soul. Think about that. Your soul is eternal. That means your friends can have a huge influence on you eternally.

Will Smith was right: choose your friends wisely. Surround yourself with people who support your faith in God. If you've ever been in a difficult situation, you know how nice it is to have a good friend there who can help you out. Imagine what it's like to have a friend who will support you in your faith:

- Shady friends invite you somewhere where you know you'll get into trouble. A good friend invites you somewhere where you can have fun without doing something stupid.
- When you're tempted to do something like cheat or look at inappropriate pictures, a good friend encourages you to make the right choice and doesn't make you feel stupid for being tempted.
- If you have an opportunity to stand up for your faith, your friend stands with you, representing Christ with you.

FINAL THOUGHTS

Be careful who you choose as friends. Think about your five best friends right now. Do they encourage you in your faith . . .*or drag you away?*

LEARN TO COOK. THE LADIES LOVE A MAN WHO KNOWS HIS WAY AROUND THE KITCHEN!

THIS IS ONE PIECE OF ADVICE THAT WILL HELP YOU now *and* in the future!

Every guy should learn a few basic cooking skills. Why?

- Like most people, you'll probably live on your own at least once in your life, and you'll need to know how to prepare a meal. Man cannot live on microwave meals alone.
- Learning to cook a meal *now* gives you the opportunity to help your parents by cooking dinner for the family every once in a while. If you really want to impress your parents, tell them you'll prepare supper next Tuesday.
- Imagine this: it's your third date with a girl, and you invite her to your house to meet your parents. . .only, *you cook*! What girl isn't going to be impressed when you prepare fresh veggies and a perfectly marinated grilled chicken breast? (Unless, of course, she's a vegetarian; then you'd better learn how to prepare wheatgrass and tofu!)

The ladies love a man who can cook!

Cooking is one of those life skills you need to know. So, next time a meal is being prepared for you, ask if you can help. Roll up your sleeves, wash your hands, read the recipe, and learn how to cut an onion (and cry). Better yet, once you look at a recipe, go to the grocery store with Mom or Dad and shop for the ingredients you'll need. Then come home and prepare the meal from scratch. While you're at it, learn how to set a table and how to wash dishes when you're through.

Learn the difference between baking (where the ingredient measurements are often exact) and cooking (where the ingredients may be measured in pinches or handfuls). Cooking allows you to sprinkle salt to taste. With baking. . .just follow the recipe. Either way, preparing meals can be a lot of fun.

GO AHEAD, ANSWER. . .

+ What is your favorite home-cooked meal?

+ Do you know how to make this meal?

+ Who typically prepares this meal in your home?

+ How would he or she respond if you asked to help prepare it?

+ What meals do you know how to cook right now? (No, a bowl of cereal doesn't count. . .but toast does!)

+ How many meals can you prepare? (Not including instant microwave meals!)

+ What other meals would you like to learn how to prepare?

FINAL THOUGHTS

I don't know a woman alive who isn't impressed with a man who cooks and cleans up after a meal. This simple skill is appreciated by everyone. Make the effort to learn how to cook. You'll be glad you did.

7.

WISDOM IS PAVED WITH PAST MISTAKES. DON'T MISS THE OPPORTUNITY TO LEARN FROM YOUR BLUNDERS.

THIS PRINCIPLE IS SIMPLE: LEARN FROM YOUR MISTAKES. In other words, when you mess up, take note of *why*. . .and figure out how to navigate the situation better next time.

Let's say it's a Thursday night and your friends are all hanging out together and having fun. You want to hang with them, but you have a big English test the next day and you know you need to stay home and study. You decide to skip studying and hang out with your friends instead.

Hanging out was a blast. . .*for a few hours.* But soon you're back home and the pressure of the test is weighing heavily on your shoulders. You try to study really quick before falling asleep, but it's late, so you doze off. The next day you take the test and you do horribly. You get a D and your grade in the class drops an entire letter grade. To make matters worse, your car insurance, which was cheap because of a "good student" discount, increases by $32 a month (yes, this is based on a true story) because you missed the discount by one grade.

All that for a couple of hours of fun one night?

Was it worth it? Was it really that much fun? Couldn't you have studied Thursday and invited all your friends over to your house on Friday or Saturday night?

Here's the point: you made a mistake. So what? It happens. You don't become a fool until you repeat the same mistake.

Learn from your mistake and avoid the pain next time.

A month later, your friend calls you again, but this time it's a Tuesday night and you have math homework. What are you going to say?

1. "Sure. Count me in. Who cares about grades anyway!" (Or the cost of my car insurance. . .or the college I want to attend. . .or my future!)
2. "Sounds fun, but I can't tonight. What are you doing Friday?"

Don't repeat the same mistake.

GO AHEAD, ANSWER. . .

+ What are some past mistakes you have made?

+ What were the consequences?

+ How could you have avoided these mistakes in the first place?

+ Did you repeat the mistake?

+ What is the best way to avoid repeating this mistake?

+ What are some of the benefits of avoiding this mistake in the future?

FINAL THOUGHTS

Everyone makes mistakes. Life is full of situations where we make poor choices, only to look back later and regret our decisions. Don't beat yourself up. But don't miss the opportunity to learn from the experience. Wisdom is paved with past mistakes.

8

LOSING YOUR TEMPER FEELS REALLY GOOD... FOR ABOUT SEVENTEEN SECONDS. KEEPING YOUR COOL FEELS EVEN BETTER... AND FOR A LOT LONGER.

PEOPLE ARE FRUSTRATING.

It's true. No matter where you go, you'll run into people who are annoying, maddening, even downright infuriating. It's natural to feel angry or irritated in these situations. The question is, what do you do with those feelings?

For example: When you learn to drive, you will frequently encounter selfish people who frustrate you on the road. You might be driving on a road where traffic is merging from two lanes down to one. Everyone takes turns merging together— until it's your turn. All of a sudden, someone in the other lane speeds up, cuts you off, and merges in front of you—basically cutting in line.

There's never a policeman around when this happens, so no one enforces it. Now you have to stare at this idiot's bumper for the next few minutes—the jerk who just cut you off!

It's completely normal to be frustrated in this situation. The question is, how will you deal with these feelings? Which is the correct response?

A. At the next stoplight, pull out the crowbar you keep under your seat and take out all your aggression on this guy's windshield!

B. Don't use violence, just yell at the guy, curse, and call him names that you learned in the locker room in middle school.

C. Don't do anything at all. Just bottle it all up inside, letting it fester inside of you. In your mind, pretend you are slowly torturing him with a pair of pliers.

D. Laugh to yourself and say, "There he is." Knowing that you're bound to encounter a few of these people every day. Tell yourself, "That's frustrating, but I'm not going to let it affect the rest of my day."

Unfortunately, choices A, B, and C all have pretty nasty consequences, from high blood pressure to jail. Choice D, on the other hand, allows you to feel angry but helps you deal with the anger in a healthy way.

The Bible provides some pretty shrewd wisdom on the subject of anger. In Ephesians 4:26–27, Paul writes:

> *"Don't sin by letting anger control you." Don't let the sun go down while you are still angry, for anger gives a foothold to the devil.*

GO AHEAD, ANSWER. . .

+ According to the verse, is anger wrong?

+ According to the verse, when does anger become sin?

+ Give an example of how anger can control us.

+ What are some ways to avoid being *controlled* by anger when we *feel* angry?

+ The verse tells us not to let the sun go down while we're still angry— in other words, don't hold on to your anger. What happens when we hold on to anger for a long time?

+ Why would a guy decide to put himself into a torture chamber of bitterness and anger?

Anger is natural. Anger can even be good, such as when we become upset by mistreatment or injustice. Even God gets angry. But we need to keep anger from controlling us.

So how do we fight the grip of anger?

The key is giving God control. When you're feeling angry or frustrated, pray and ask God to help you handle it. "Because if I handle it myself, God, I'll probably hurt someone."

If this sounds difficult. . .you're right. . .if you're trying to do it on your own. That's why it's a good idea to turn to God so He can help you. The more you read about Jesus and how He treated people, how He forgave people and loved people. . . the more you'll know how to respond in different situations. More importantly, you'll know how to accept God's help and let Him respond through you.

FINAL THOUGHTS

Read Galatians 5:16–26. In this little passage of scripture, Paul describes the difference between someone who lives his life giving into every urge, compared to someone who lives life with the strength provided by God's Spirit. Which list do you want to follow?

It's your choice. It all comes down to who you put in charge.

9.

LEARN A SKILL THAT WOULD HELP YOU SURVIVE A ZOMBIE APOCALYPSE.

WHAT WOULD YOU DO IF YOU DIDN'T HAVE ACCESS to bottled water. . .or even water from your faucet or hose. Where could you get clean water?

What if you had to hunt or grow your own food? What would you eat? How would you prepare it?

Where would you go for shelter if you were out on the street? Can you make your own shelter?

These are skills you might need to know during a zombie apocalypse.

Okay. . .I admit it; chances are slim to none that corpses are going to start walking the earth. And it's not a good idea to plague ourselves with worry about how we would survive if the world were coming to an end. But it also wouldn't hurt to learn a few survival skills in case you're ever in an emergency situation.

GO AHEAD, ANSWER. . .

+ If you were driving across the country with your family and your car broke down, would you know what to do? Do you know how to change a flat tire? Do you keep water, food, and blankets in the car?

+ If you went on a hike and got lost, would you know how to build a shelter? Would you know where to find clean water?

+ If you became trapped in a snowstorm, what would you do for warmth? Do you know how to keep warm in a car? Do you know how to build a snow cave? Do you know how to build a fire if you don't have matches?

+ If you were lost at sea, would you know how to survive on the ocean? Do you know how to fish? Do you know how to swim? Can you navigate by using the stars?

The funny thing is, until about a hundred years ago, kids your age probably knew how to survive in most of these situations (except if zombies started walking around). The more technologically advanced our society has grown, the more spoiled and ignorant we have become.

Perhaps it wouldn't hurt to learn a few survival skills. Here are some fun options:

1. Ask your dad or other knowledgeable adult to show you how to change a tire, how to fish, and how to build a fire.

2. Go on a backpacking trip with someone trustworthy and experienced and learn to live off the land for a few days.

3. Watch survival shows on the Discovery Channel—shows where people give advice on how to be resourceful under a variety of circumstances.

4. Join a club, like the Boy Scouts, where you can learn survival skills.

5. Read a book about survival, such as *The US Military Pocket Survival Guide*; or, if you want something a little more fun, try my book *The Zombie Apocalypse Survival Guide for Teenagers*.

FINAL THOUGHTS

Let's hope you never have to escape flesh-eating creatures or survive off the land for months at a time. But chances are you'll probably have to change a flat tire, and maybe even find a food or water source in an emergency situation. Are you prepared? Maybe you should make plans to try one of the options listed above.

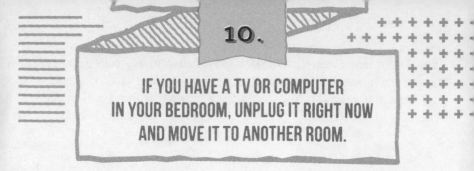

10.

IF YOU HAVE A TV OR COMPUTER IN YOUR BEDROOM, UNPLUG IT RIGHT NOW AND MOVE IT TO ANOTHER ROOM.

DO YOU HAVE ACCESS TO TV, INTERNET, OR VIDEO games in your bedroom? Yeah. . .that includes your phone. If so, it's time to make your room "connection-free."

Doctor's orders.

That's right, a few years ago, the journal *Pediatrics* posted an article advising parents to remove all the screens from their kids' bedrooms.

GO AHEAD, ANSWER. . .

+ Why do you think doctors would advise parents to remove screens from the bedroom?

+ What kinds of distractions are available on TV today?

+ What kinds of distractions are available on a computer?

+ What kinds of distractions are available on a smartphone?

+ Why are young people more vulnerable to these distractions in their bedrooms?

Think about it. There's a huge difference between watching TV in the living room while Mom's cooking dinner and when you are watching TV in your bedroom late at night with the door shut. The privacy of a bedroom can create a very vulnerable atmosphere.

Let's talk specifically about lust.

Sadly, TV offers plenty of sexual temptations. Pay-per-view channels often show sex and nudity (especially at night), and even broadcast channels show some sensual, racy images. Let's be honest: sometimes these sensual images get us guys thinking about sex; and if we allow ourselves the temptation, it's easy to start lusting after some of those images.

Back in New Testament times, some people thought that lusting was no big deal. They figured if they didn't actually commit adultery, then they were all right. Jesus straightened them out in a hurry: "Anyone who even looks at a woman with lust has already committed adultery with her in his heart" (Matthew 5:28).

But the Bible also gives us some great advice about how to avoid this kind of sexual temptation. And it's simple, too: *RUN AWAY!*

Yes, it really says that.

> *Run from sexual sin! No other sin so clearly affects the body as this one does. For sexual immorality is a sin against your own body.* (1 Corinthians 6:18)

I find it intriguing that doctors today have come to a similar conclusion: it's better to avoid trouble before it starts. Screens in the bedroom often lead to trouble.

FINAL THOUGHTS

I realize that it might be a little scary to ask Mom or Dad, "Hey! Can you remove the computer from my room so I'm not tempted to watch porn?"

Maybe you don't have to word it like that. Most parents would be pretty impressed if their son told them, "I don't even want the temptation of having a computer in my room. Can we keep it in the family room?"

While you're at it, ask your parents to charge your phone every night. If you think that's crazy, just ask yourself honestly, *Have I ever been tempted by something on my phone at night?* Well. . .how can you "run away" from that temptation?

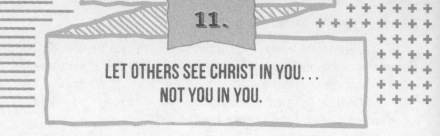

11.

LET OTHERS SEE CHRIST IN YOU. . . NOT YOU IN YOU.

IN MATTHEW 5:14–16, JESUS TELLS HIS FOLLOWERS that we are a light.

What kind of light?

Most Christians are one of two types of light: a lava lamp or a spotlight.

Lava lamps are really fun to look at. When these interesting décor items get hot, the "lava" inside begins floating and moving around in random formations. If a lava lamp were a person, it would say, "Look at me. Look at what a cool light I am. Watch me!"

Spotlights are completely different. Instead of drawing attention to themselves, they point to something more important and draw everyone's attention to it. If a spotlight were a person, it would say, "Look at Him. He is worth looking at. Let me illuminate Him!"

Which kind of light are you?

Some Christians think they are a lava lamp. "Look at me. I'm such a good Christian. I give money to the poor. I'm a leader at my church. I don't listen to that bad music. Look at what a good Christian I am!"

But when Jesus told us to let our light shine, He didn't ask us to be lava lamps.

Here's what Jesus says in Matthew 5:16:

> *In the same way, let your good deeds shine out for all to see,*
> *so that everyone will praise your heavenly Father.*

GO AHEAD, ANSWER. . .

+ According to the verse, why should we let our good deeds shine?

+ Where is the proper focus of attention?

+ What kind of light is the person in this verse, a lava lamp ("Look at me"), or a spotlight ("Look at Him")?

+ When people see us doing good deeds, why would they praise God?

The tough thing about being a light for Jesus is the temptation to illuminate ourselves. That's called *pride*. Pride says, "Look at me. Look at the good thing *I* just did."

Maybe it's not that obvious. Maybe we just make sure others notice when we do something good. Perhaps we draw attention when someone else does something bad and make it clear, "I would never do that."

"Look at me!"

What do people see when they look at you? Do they see a lava lamp—shining a whole lot of *you*? Or do they see a spotlight—you pointing to Jesus in everything you do?

FINAL THOUGHTS

The apostle Paul knew about our human struggle with pride. That's probably why he said this:

You see, we don't go around preaching about ourselves. We preach that Jesus Christ is Lord, and we ourselves are your servants for Jesus' sake. (2 Corinthians 4:5)

How can you reflect Jesus this week?

12.

DON'T UNDERESTIMATE A FEMALE'S SENSE OF SMELL.

I DON'T KNOW WHY SO MANY GUYS ARE OBLIVIOUS TO this, but it's a secret that only a few seem to recognize: good breath and a nice cologne go a long way.

I think we're too quick to assume that girls think just like guys do. *Wrong!*

Guys are visual creatures. If our eyes see something sexy. . .there's no turning it off. The other senses don't even matter. *Who cares if she just went on a five-mile run and smells like sweat! She's gorgeous!* Actually. . .she doesn't even have to be gorgeous. . .she's wearing short shorts! *Guys ain't picky.*

Girls are *way* different. If a guy is good looking, sure, that helps; but that doesn't seal the deal. Other senses matter—a gentle touch, a caring voice. . . and, yes, an alluring smell. Or, at least, *the lack of a repugnant smell.*

Guys, how we smell matters. So, consider these suggestions:

- Shower every day. Don't be fooled into thinking that every other day is fine. It's not. The moment you hit puberty, your body starts to excrete all kinds of sweaty fluids in every crevice. Bacteria feast on this stuff and then excrete their own waste. . .and that *stinks*. Shower with soap and shampoo. Yes, this sounds basic, but a lot of guys don't do it (a lot of *single* guys).

- Use deodorant. It's cheap and it's easy to use. Just slap some in your armpits and be careful not to get a white streak on your nice clean shirt. . .which leads me to my next tip.

- Wash your clothes! Don't wear your favorite shirt five days in a row. In most cases, once is enough before it needs to be laundered again. Especially if you live where it's humid (that's you, Houston). There are times where you might shower, put on a shirt, and wear it around the house for a few hours, then take it off before bed. Then. . .maybe. . .it might be good to wear one more time. When in doubt, toss it in the washing machine. Why? Smell matters!

- Try a little cologne. Grab your sister, your cousin, or your chemistry partner (someone female) and ask her to go to the store with you to smell colognes. Yes, they're pretty expensive. But you only need one or two pumps of a spray bottle (don't use too much) each morning after your shower.
- Brush your teeth and carry gum. Bad breath is a killer. No one likes talking with a guy who smells like he just ate garlic onion fries.

FINAL THOUGHTS

Let me be very clear. I'm not suggesting we should *worry* about what others think about us. We don't need to obsess about our smell. There are far greater things in life than smelling good. Nevertheless, we don't want to be so lazy that we torture the people sitting next to us in the car. Showering, brushing teeth, and wearing cologne are simple gestures that others will appreciate. . .*especially when you meet the right girl.*

13.

YOU'LL NEVER PLEASE EVERYONE, AND YOU'LL NEVER PLEASE YOURSELF COMPLETELY... SO SEEK TO PLEASE YOUR CREATOR. IT'S MIND-BENDINGLY FULFILLING!

"I'M DOING WHATEVER OTHERS WANT, OR WHATEVER I want. . .so why am I so miserable?"

If you've ever tried making everyone happy, you've probably found that it's an impossible task. You can never please everyone. And if you've ever tried living completely for yourself, then you quickly discovered that selfish efforts lead to a very lonely and sad existence.

So what's the answer?

Jesus said it plainly and simply in Matthew 6:33:

> *"Seek the Kingdom of God above all else, and live righteously, and he will give you everything you need."*

GO AHEAD, ANSWER. . .

+ According to the verse, what are we supposed to seek?

+ What does it mean to seek the "kingdom of God"?

+ How does the verse tell us to live?

+ What does it mean to live righteously?

+ What would that look like in your life?

+ What does God say He'll give us when we live righteously?

+ What are some of the "needs" that God will provide?

+ What are some examples of things we might not *need* right now. . . even though we might want them?

It's amazing. It almost doesn't make sense. But it's true. If we live to please others, we'll always disappoint someone. If we live for ourselves, we're selfish slimeballs and we'll have no friends. But when we live to please God, serving Him and doing right simply because of our love for Him. . .everything else falls into place.

Don't get me wrong. I'm not saying life will always be simple and drama-free. Life always has its share of adversity. But when you're living to please God, He'll help you through it. And when you have God's love flowing through you, it will help you in your relationships with others!

FINAL THOUGHTS

Give it a try. Start today and give it twenty-four hours. During that time, try to do what's right in every situation. Don't work to impress others, and don't live selfishly for yourself. Instead, pray and tell God you want to please Him in everything you do. I can't promise that the people around will respond perfectly. They probably won't. But that's okay. . .you're not trying to impress them anyway. You are only concerned about an Audience of One. Seek to please Him.

REMEMBER, THE GIRL YOU'RE CHECKING OUT IS SOMEONE'S DAUGHTER!

I'LL NEVER FORGET THE FIGHT BETWEEN BRIAN AND Steve during my sophomore year in high school.

Three days a week, we had a weights class during second period. This meant we had to dress down into our PE clothes in the locker room. It's amazing what a young man can learn from the other guys in a locker room. It's probably the one place where guys will talk about whatever they want. Our PE teacher was never around, and the girls were in their own locker room. So this left a bunch of fourteen- and fifteen-year-old guys unsupervised for about ten minutes while they changed clothes.

I rarely remember a conversation that wasn't rated R. . .or XXX.

Brian was one of the worst. He would kiss his girlfriend good-bye and whisper sweet words in her ear before class started, and then he'd walk into the locker room and tell us all what he planned to do with her that night. . .*in explicit detail*. He and several other guys often bragged about what they had done with various girls (usually girls we knew), and even rated them by their looks (with and without clothes) and their "performance."

One day the conversation came around to a girl whom Brian said he hoped to get his hands on. He made a few comments about this girl's body and what he planned to do to her. . .and that's when it happened. Brian didn't know that he was talking about Steve's sister.

Voices were raised and soon fists were flying. I have never seen such a beating. Steve was hitting Brian with such anger.

What made this situation bizarre was that Steve had often joked with Brian about other girls, their bodies, and every sexual act you could imagine. But as soon as Brian mentioned Steve's sister. . .everything changed. Steve's sister was off-limits.

+ Why did Steve fight with Brian?

+ Steve laughed and talked bad about girls with Brian every day. Why was it different when it was his sister?

+ Should it be any different? Explain.

+ Was Brian worse for talking bad about Steve's sister?

+ Is it okay to lust after girls and treat them like objects. . .as long as you don't know them?

+ What are ways that guys commonly lust after girls and treat them like objects today?

The world would love to convince us that girls are just sex objects. In most beer commercials, music videos, and sporting events, women are often made out to be one thing: *eye candy*. Let's face it: men love to look at pretty girls (we talked about that in #3).

Why does our response change when it's a girl we know and love?

How would you like it if guys were lusting and talking about explicit sexual acts with your sister or your mom?

FINAL THOUGHTS

Next time, think twice before you look at a girl like she's a sex object. That's not only lust (which we know is wrong), but she's also someone's sister. . .someone's daughter.

And, trust me: you don't want Steve beating you up!

15.

PROFANE TALK PROVIDES OTHERS WITH A GLIMPSE OF WHAT'S SEEPING OUT OF YOUR HEART.

WHEN MY DAUGHTER WAS IN THIRD GRADE, SHE discovered the word *hell*.

She came into my room one day and asked me, "Daddy? Is *hell* a bad word?"

"That's a good question, Ashley," I responded. "Some people might think so. If you are talking about the place, then it's not bad; but if you're saying it just to fill in an empty space in a sentence, then a lot of people might be offended by it."

Ashley thought for a moment. "So, if I say, 'What the hell!' it's bad?"

"Well, many people don't like that use of the word. So, yes, I don't think you should say it."

Three days later, Ashley was in her room and she exclaimed, "Where the hell is my binder?"

"Ashley!" I yelled from the other room.

After a long pause, she added, "I was talking about the place."

That's when I decided that I'd give her a punishment that I knew her brother and sister both hated. I made her write a one-page paper about profane language.

Once again, I probably should have been more specific. About twenty minutes later, she turned it into me. I glanced at the title—"Bad Words"—and began to read: *There are many bad words I shouldn't say. Here are some of them. . . .*

With that, she listed every bad word she knew, starting with the f-word, and moving down the list.

That was seven years ago. She's still grounded today.

Profane talk is pretty common today. Our friends at school use it, our favorite movie has it, even people at church might use some words that our grandma never used. And to make matters more confusing, some people are offended by words that others don't mind at all.

How do we know what's right?

In Ephesians 5:4, Paul provides a nice little reminder:

> *Obscene stories, foolish talk, and coarse jokes—these are not for you. Instead, let there be thankfulness to God.*

GO AHEAD, ANSWER. . .

+ According to the verse, what words are "not for you"?

+ What are examples of these three kinds of talk?

+ Why do you think Paul wants us to avoid this?

I like Paul. Before Paul met Jesus, he was a legalist. That means he was worried about a long list of "don't do this" and "don't do that." But when Paul met Jesus, everything changed. Paul no longer worried about acting religious. Instead, he focused on putting our trust in Jesus and allowing Him to change us from the inside out.

When we allow Jesus to change our attitudes on the inside, God's love seeps out of us in our words and actions.

FINAL THOUGHTS

If your words are constantly obscene, rude, or belittling to others. . .you might want to ask yourself what's going on in your heart.

How we talk provides others a glimpse of what's inside us.

16.

GUYS WHO TRASH-TALK USUALLY DO SO BECAUSE THEY'RE INSECURE AND SELF-DOUBTING.

NOBODY LIKES A BULLY. SADLY, THERE'S NOT A SCHOOL campus in America that doesn't have one.

Is it you?

That's one of the funny things about bullies. Bullies never see themselves as bullies. You'd think they'd recognize themselves when they see the archetypal bully represented in every movie and TV program about teenagers. Every show seems to feature a bully who pushes around smaller people, calling them names, and making their lives miserable.

Is that the only kind of bully?

What about the subtle bullying that goes on every day by so many? Someone ugly, different, poor, or even someone truly irritating walks by in the hallway and you exchange a laugh with your friends. You don't even think about it as bullying but it's a clear gesture saying, "What is wrong with that guy? What a loser."

Why do we do that to others?

Most of us do it because it makes us feel better about ourselves when we put others down. If we laugh at someone who's not as handsome, intelligent, or fashionable as we fancy ourselves, we feel better about ourselves. When we "step" on others, we raise ourselves up to feel better. We seek affirmation from others. We never verbalize it, but we're basically asking, "I'm better than he is, right?"

Maybe we should consider Paul's advice in Philippians 2:3–4:

Don't be selfish; don't try to impress others. Be humble, thinking of others as better than yourselves. Don't look out only for your own interests, but take an interest in others, too.

GO AHEAD, ANSWER. . .

+ Give an example of a time when you were selfish.

+ Give an example of trying to impress others.

+ How can we think of others as better as than ourselves?

+ How can you take more of an interest in others?

+ How can you practice humility today, tomorrow, and this week?

TRY THIS. . .

+ Instead of teasing the kid who is sitting alone, sit next to him.

+ Don't pick a winning team in PE class. Pick a few of the guys who are always picked last.

+ Ask other people questions about themselves instead of talking about yourself!

+ If someone starts talking trash about someone, bring up something good about the person instead. "You might think that, but I happen to like Eugene. He's an amazing cello player!" (Warning: you might get beat up for this one.)

You have the power to lift up someone else this week.
How are you going to do it?

FINAL THOUGHTS

It's easy to step on others. Sometimes it slips out so quickly we don't even catch ourselves doing it. But we are stomping on others to raise ourselves up.

Perhaps we're not the school bully who picks on everyone else; but maybe, if we're honest with ourselves, we do make fun of others.

God has a different plan for us. When we connect with God and let His love flow through us, His love flows out to others in humility and selflessness.

17.

GO AN ENTIRE DAY WITHOUT USING ANYTHING ELECTRONIC.

"I BET YOU CAN'T GO EVEN ONE DAY WITHOUT THAT stupid phone."

"Oh yeah?"

Taylor hit the power switch and put his phone on the counter. He wasn't about to let his mom be right.

Every argument in the last three weeks between Taylor and his mom revolved around Taylor's phone.

"Stop texting at the dinner table."

"Turn your phone off; it's time to get to bed."

"Stop letting that phone interrupt your homework."

"You're addicted to that thing!"

Taylor enjoyed his phone, but he thought it was ludicrous to say he was "addicted" to it. There's a big difference between enjoyment and addiction. Taylor decided to prove his mother wrong.

"Yeah, but you'll just go log on to your computer or watch TV," she continued. "It's the same thing. You're addicted to screens."

"I'm not addicted!" Taylor insisted. "Watch."

That's how it started. Taylor began his twenty-four-hour "gadget fast."

Lots of teenagers like Taylor have tried it. *Not all have succeeded.*

Have you ever tried taking a break from all your gadgets?

Electronic gadgets aren't bad. They can be great tools for communication, organization, research, and countless other tasks. But our world is growing increasingly dependent on these gadgets. A 2013 study revealed that the average American spends two hours and thirty-eight minutes a day on his or her smartphone alone.[5] That's a lot of time staring at that pocket-sized screen.

How addicted are you to your gadgets? Do your gadgets interfere with important elements in your life?

+ Do you ever find yourself in a room with your friends but engaged with your phone instead of in conversation with the people in front of you?

+ Do you have important conversations via text instead of face-to-face?

+ Do you ever find yourself wasting time looking at funny pictures and videos when you're supposed to be doing something else?

+ Do you wear headphones even around others?

There's nothing wrong with texting, looking at funny pictures, or wearing headphones. But sometimes these actions distract us from the people around us. When this happens, we might want to take a break from our gadgets and discipline ourselves to give the people around us greater priority than our electronic devices.

If you're thinking to yourself, *I don't have a problem with my phone*, or, *I don't let my gadgets interfere with the people around me*, then go ahead, give it a try for just twenty-four hours. Go on a one-day gadget fast. Devote an entire day to face-to-face conversations, reading, or outdoor activities. Then take an honest assessment of how the day turned out. If it goes well. . .get a few friends to join you the next time. . .*and this time try it for a week*!

I went on a media fast for a month last year with my family. No TV, movies, music, or recreational Internet and texting (we still used the Internet and phones for business). It was very difficult at first—but then something happened. We began spending a lot more time together just talking and doing creative activities. We read more and enjoyed the outdoors. We played with our cats. . .and laughed a lot.

My three teenagers even admitted it was a great experience.

FINAL THOUGHTS

What about you? Do you have the guts to try a gadget fast for just twenty-four hours?

Give it a try. I think you'll be surprised with the results.

18.

WHEN A GIRL WALKS BY...
KEEP LOOKING FORWARD.

IT HAPPENS ALL THE TIME. A GIRL WALKS BY A GROUP of guys, and all their heads turn.

I guess it wouldn't be so bad if all the guys were thinking, *What a nice young lady. I wonder if she's good at math or enjoys a good game of checkers.*

Sadly, most guys who turn their heads are thinking thoughts they are glad no one else can see or hear.

GO AHEAD, ANSWER. . .

+ What are most guys thinking about when they turn their heads to look at a girl?

+ When does *admiring* become *lusting*?

+ Read Matthew 5:28. What does this verse say about lust?

+ What is the best practice when a pretty girl walks by?

It's not bad to notice pretty girls. Just don't let "noticing" turn into lusting.

If you're attracted to pretty girls, you have something to look forward to when you get married. God has created something amazing just for married couples. It's called sexual intimacy.

The world is so in love with the idea of sexual intimacy that many people will do anything they can to convince themselves that it's okay to pursue it with anyone they meet. But that isn't God's design. God created us to share our intimate selves with only one person—our spouse. When the time comes, you can be unashamedly naked with your wife and enjoy sex with her—exclusively. Like any special gift, sexual intimacy is a treasure to be closely guarded.

FINAL THOUGHTS

So, don't try to sneak a peek when a beautiful girl walks by. Sure, it's natural to notice her. But don't turn your head, and don't turn your thoughts. Don't go any further than noticing. Instead, pray and say, "God, I'm looking forward to the naked girl you have for me someday. Help me to wait for her."

God will honor that prayer. . .and He'll give you the strength to keep looking forward when pretty girls pass by.

19

BEING IN SHAPE SHOWS SELF-CONTROL AND COMMITMENT. . .AND GIRLS LIKE ALL THREE!

JIM WAS A GOOD FATHER, HUSBAND, AND FRIEND. Those closest to him described him as warm, caring, and funny. Everyone loved Jim.

Jim never exercised and he ate whatever he wanted.

"It was part of what made Jim. . .Jim," his friends would say. He loved food and always knew the best places to eat.

Jim died at fifty-two years old.

A poor diet and lack of exercise might seem like no big deal, but the consequences are lurking like a flock of vultures. Name it: diabetes, heart problems, obesity. . .even death.

French fries aren't evil, but they should be eaten in moderation. It all comes down to self-control.

Proverbs 25:28 says it about as simply as it can be said:

A person without self-control is like a city with broken-down walls.

GO AHEAD, ANSWER. . .

+ What is self-control?

+ To what does Proverbs compare self-control?

+ Why do you think this verse makes this comparison?

+ Why is self-control important in the area of diet and exercise?

+ What are some ways you might need to show self-control in these areas?

I'm not recommending that you start obsessing over your body. I'm not suggesting that you try to get abs like Taylor Lautner's. I'm just suggesting that you make some healthy eating and exercise habits. Besides. . .girls like a guy who's in shape.

Try these commonly known healthy exercise and eating tips:

- Get at least fifty minutes of cardio exercise at least five days a week (cardio is when your heart has to beat faster).
- Eat protein with every meal (common proteins are meat or beans).
- Eat multiple servings of fruits and vegetables every day.
- Work your muscles out several days a week. You don't need fancy weights; you can do amazing muscle workouts with just push-ups, lunges, and various sit-ups.
- Drink eight glasses of water a day. It's good for you, and it makes you full so you eat less junk.
- Drink fewer soft drinks. The fewer the better. Definitely not more than one a day (three a week would be better. . .zero a week would be best).
- Don't snack after dinner. Calories consumed after dinner don't help.

FINAL THOUGHTS

Try some of these tips this week. Being in shape shows self-control and commitment. . .and girls like all three!

20.

REMEMBER, YOU ARE MUCH SMARTER THAN YOUR DOG!

WOULDN'T IT BE NICE TO LIVE OUR LIVES WITHOUT any limits, indulging in whatever we wanted?

What if we did whatever we felt like at any given moment?

As enticing as that may sound, if we let it play out to the end, it never works. Every action has a reaction. Every choice has a consequence. The question is always this: Are you smart enough to look beyond the moment?

I love dogs. When my wife and I were first married, we owned two amazing Labradors. Like many dogs, the highlight of their day was dinnertime. The routine was simple. I'd walk outside to the dog food bin we kept on the side of the house. I'd open the lid, fill their bowls, and set the bowls in front of them.

The dogs quickly learned this routine. Every night when I walked toward the food bin, they'd grow excited, running over to me, wagging their tails, panting and salivating like true Pavlovian dogs. They'd carefully watch as I unlatched the lid and scooped two cups of dog food into each bowl. As I set the bowls down, they could hardly contain themselves. Usually, they'd begin devouring their meal before the bowl even hit the ground. Most often, they'd finish their portion in less than thirty seconds and look up at me like, *That's it? Really?*

Two cups was what the vet recommended for their weight. Any more and they could become overweight and experience a host of problems. So, every night I limited them to two scoops. Every night they hounded me as I prepared the food, and then lapped it up in under a minute.

One night I walked to the side of the house to feed them and they didn't run over to greet me. I called their names, but they didn't emerge from their doghouse or around the corner. Just as I began to wonder if they were missing, I noticed the food bin on its side, with kibble spilling out of the opening. The bin was nearly empty, which was odd. . .I had just filled it earlier in the week with a huge forty-pound bag. I was not only missing two dogs. . .I was missing a large amount of dog food.

That's when I heard it—a distinct whine coming from the doghouse.

I called to them. "Alpine? Roxy? Is that you?"

Alpine poked her head out of the doghouse slowly. She didn't look well.

"Alpine? Are you okay, girl? Come here."

Both dogs waddled out of the doghouse. . .*two of the fattest dogs I'd ever seen!* They were stuffed like sausages and looked ready to burst at any moment.

The dogs moaned with every step. They were literally in pain.

I almost fell to the ground laughing.

Apparently, I hadn't fastened the lid to the bin the night before, and the dogs had tipped the bin and pushed open the lid. I would have paid money to witness it, because they probably thought they had struck gold!

I wonder how long they ate when the food first spilled out. Did they take a break? Or did they just keep going until no more food would fit down the hatch?

Regardless, the poor pups were suffering now. They indulged until they couldn't eat another morsel. They had lived for the moment with no regard for the future, and now the future had come calling.

I found their shortsightedness intriguing. I guess I shouldn't be surprised. They're dogs, not humans. Dogs don't reason. When the bin tipped, Alpine didn't warn Roxy, "Now remember, Roxy, if we eat too much, we'll regret it later. Limit yourself."

They didn't consider any future consequences. Those dogs love food, and with no boundaries in place, they consumed until it hurt.

Isn't it a relief that humans aren't as shortsighted as dogs? We have the ability to reason, so we'd never indulge in something that we know would hurt us. . .*right*?

Sadly. . .not always.

GO AHEAD, ANSWER. . .

+ What are ways that teenagers commonly "live for the moment" with no regard for consequences?

+ What are some of the consequences they face?

+ In what ways do you sometimes act without foresight?

+ What consequences have you experienced?

+ How can you avoid this in the future?

FINAL THOUGHTS

The world would love to convince us that "living for the moment" is fun. In actuality, it often *is* fun. . .for the moment. But not for the long run.

Think about that for a second. What would you rather live for—a temporary little moment or the long run? Think about those words: *moment* vs. *long run*. The word *moment* even sounds quick and fleeting, but we often tend to indulge in moments, with no regard for the long run.

My dogs had the same problem. Perhaps you should consider this: *you're waaaaaaaaaay smarter than my dogs!*

21

GO OUT OF YOUR WAY TO SAY HI TO AN ELDERLY PERSON. INTRODUCE YOURSELF. START A CONVERSATION. . .AND LISTEN.

ELLA MAY WAS BORN IN MISSOURI IN 1913, THE YEAR after the *Titanic* sank. When she was a young woman, she married Ray, and the two of them survived on the small income he earned working construction.

When the Great Depression hit, Ray and May moved across the country to California, where Ray's brother had found work in a cannery. Ray and May both got jobs canning peaches and lived in a small trailer near the California coast. These were tough times financially, but happy times. Ray and May always had each other.

The Great Depression passed, and the war brought jobs. Ray and May moved back to Missouri, and Ray developed his skills as a contractor, building custom homes. They started a family with the birth of a baby girl. Ray's business grew, and so did their daughter. She eventually went away to college and got married. It was then that Ray got cancer. He passed away when May was fifty-four, leaving her by herself.

May spent the next forty years as a widow. Her daughter's family tried their best to keep her near, but sometimes their jobs required them to move to different cities.

May spent almost half her adult life alone in an empty house.

There are people like May all over our country. . .there's probably someone like her living just down the street from you. Like May, they have stories of good times and relationships past. . .but no one to talk to.

Take a peek at what James says about widows:

> *Pure and genuine religion in the sight of God the Father means caring for orphans and widows in their distress and refusing to let the world corrupt you.* (James 1:27)

GO AHEAD, ANSWER. . .

+ According to the verse, whom are we supposed to care for?

+ Why does James call caring for orphans and widows "pure and genuine religion"?

+ How can teenagers care for widows and orphans?

+ Where in your community might you meet some elderly people?

+ How would you begin a conversation with an elderly person?

FINAL THOUGHTS

Most people will someday be old themselves, and many might spend some years alone. Wouldn't it be nice to have someone to talk with?

Ella May was my grandmother. We finally lived in the same city when I was a teenager. She loved it whenever my brother and I would visit her. She often told my mom that it made her week.

Sadly, when I look back on my time with her, it was sporadic and infrequent. She spent most of her time alone.

Is there someone lonely near you? Why don't you stop by and introduce yourself this week? Mow their lawn. Pull weeds in their yard. Ask to hear their stories. Maybe someone will do the same for you someday.

22

MEMORIZE SCRIPTURE.

THE WORLD IS FULL OF LIES, AND WE'LL SLOWLY START to believe them if we don't know the truth.

I can't say it any simpler than that. When we saturate ourselves with the opinions of the world day after day, the lies begin to sound like truth. That's one of the reasons it's so important to stay anchored to the truth.

Think about TV today. Most shows we watch are pretty clear at communicating some big lies:

- Sex is something you do with someone right away or after only a few dates.
- Getting drunk is something you should do to celebrate something or if you're depressed or just for fun.
- Lying is something we should do whenever it helps us get something we want.

The list goes on. Sadly, all of these practices are clearly against God's design. Furthermore, they have grave consequences (and the TV shows don't always show that).

How are we going to know this if we aren't immersing ourselves in the truth from God's Word?

One of the greatest ways to remember the truth is by memorizing it. Memorizing scripture helps you keep the truth always within reach.

Joshua 1:8 talks about the importance of studying the Bible:

> *"Study this Book of Instruction continually. Meditate on it day and night so you will be sure to obey everything written in it. Only then will you prosper and succeed in all you do."*

GO AHEAD, ANSWER. . .

+ What are we supposed to do continually?

+ What does *continually* mean?

+ What are we supposed to do day and night?

+ Why should we meditate on God's Word day and night? (Hint: The verse says, "so you will be sure to. . .")

+ Why does the book of Joshua say that studying God's Word will make us prosperous and successful? What does it mean by that?

+ How can studying the Bible help you day to day?

FINAL THOUGHTS

Think about what you have learned from this "Guy's Guide" so far. Think of all the scriptures you've read that make so much sense. Think of all the truth in those words.

What if you started taking these verses and memorizing them? You can start small—just memorize one of these scripture passages per week. The length of the verse doesn't matter. Just keep the truth close at hand. After all, *lies are lurking around every corner.*

23.

> # NEXT TIME YOU WANT TO SPEND $30 ON A NEW SHIRT, BUY A $3 SHIRT AT THE LOCAL THRIFT SHOP AND SPEND $27 ON A HOMELESS PERSON.

As Jesus looked up, he saw the rich putting their gifts into the temple treasury. He also saw a poor widow put in two very small copper coins. "Truly I tell you," he said, "this poor widow has put in more than all the others. All these people gave their gifts out of their wealth; but she out of her poverty put in all she had to live on." (Luke 21:1–4 NIV)

WHAT WOULD GENEROUS GIVING LOOK LIKE IN YOUR world? Which of your possessions would be really difficult to give up? A video game? A pair of shoes? Your phone? Can you imagine giving up one of these items?

Don't get me wrong. I'm not trying to suggest that possessions are bad, but God wants His followers to be willing to make sacrifices to help others. What would be a big sacrifice for you?

What about your popularity? Would you be willing to sacrifice that to help someone in need? Would you be willing to give the shirt off your back?

Here's why I say "your shirt." It's like this:

Four girls circle together in the noisy school hallway. "Did you see him? He's so cute!"

"Where is he?"

"Over there, in the Adidas shirt, next to the guy in the American Eagle sweater and the short guy in the Abercrombie sweatshirt."

"Wearing the Nike hat?"

"No, not the skinny guy in the Bulls jersey next to the guy in the Hollister T-shirt. . .the cute guy right there!"

It's hard to keep up with fashion anymore. Some schools are worse than others; some cliques care about it more than most. But most guys will struggle to fit in if their wardrobe is made up of shirts that Mom bought from the local truck stop.

So what's the solution?

Most young people cough up the big bucks and buy the name brands. That can mean $30 for a shirt or $50 to $100 for jeans. Smart shoppers can do a little better if they hit the right sales, but fashion still leaves a huge dent in their wallets.

That's why it would be a huge sacrifice for many guys to forgo acquiring the latest fashion to help someone in need.

Consider this:

- Instead of buying a new name-brand shirt, go to a thrift store and buy a cheap shirt. Then use the rest of your money to buy clothes or blankets for the homeless.
- Instead of buying coffee or junk food this month, buy a sandwich and a drink for someone who's homeless.
- Instead of buying that new pair of shoes you wanted, buy two cheaper pairs and give one to a homeless person.

I'm not saying that you can never buy nice clothes again, snack again, or buy those shoes you want. But I am encouraging you to try something different: for one month, make a true sacrifice to care for the needy.

FINAL THOUGHTS

Lots of people ignore the poor. Many give a little. Few give sacrificially.

Don't be like most people and give your spare change. God asks us to give much more than spare change. He wants us to give sacrificially.

What would be a sacrifice for you this month?

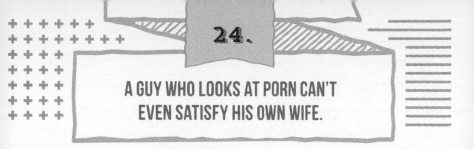

24

A GUY WHO LOOKS AT PORN CAN'T EVEN SATISFY HIS OWN WIFE.

IF YOU ENJOY LOOKING AT PORN, IT'S ALL THE SEXUAL enjoyment you're going to experience, because you won't even be able to get aroused when you want the real thing.

It sounds blunt, I know. But we live in a world that thinks porn is just no big deal. The truth is, it's easy to find, it's easy to get addicted, too. . .*and it's very difficult to quit.*

Of course, once you're addicted, the consequences start flowing. Porn hurts marriages (because most women are not happy about their husbands looking at other naked women), it hurts our relationship with God (He doesn't want us lusting), and it eventually hurts us physically. Multiple studies have shown that guys who become addicted to porn can't even get aroused when they really need to. It's like this:

1. A guy stumbles upon some naked images and likes what he sees. (God made it so we would be excited when we see a naked woman; sadly, many guys decide that one woman [their wife] isn't enough, so they also look at other women. Young guys look at women because they don't want to wait for a wife.)

2. Once a guy starts looking at naked images, he wants to see more.

3. The more he looks, the more perverse his cravings become. He desires more explicit sexual content and kinkier sex.

4. Soon he is addicted to porn.

5. After a while, his brain becomes accustomed to being bombarded with a steady flow of images and experiencing dopamine overload, and the sight of one naked girl doesn't satisfy him anymore.[6]

6. If he is involved in a monogamous relationship like a marriage, his wife doesn't arouse him anymore. She wonders what's wrong.

7. The truth comes out, and the marriage relationship often is put in jeopardy.

+ Why do you think most guys start looking at naked images of women?

+ Do you think they ever consider that it will become an addiction?

+ What are some of the consequences of becoming addicted to porn?

+ How come characters in TV shows and movies joke about porn like it's no big deal?

FINAL THOUGHTS

Porn isn't a laughing matter. Guys who become addicted often have to seek help from experts, just as if they had any other addiction.

A porn addiction typically starts when guys convince themselves that looking at sexual imagery is just "no big deal." Nothing could be further from the truth. That's why Paul warns us to "run from sexual sin!" (1 Corinthians 6:18).

If you are being tempted to look at sexual images, here are some ideas for how you can take Paul's advice and *run*:

- Tell a trusted adult friend about your struggle and ask for help.

- Remove any temptations. If you're tempted by your phone or computer at night, charge them in your parents' bedroom. Yes, this might be embarrassing to admit to them, but they should honor your request if you simply ask them, "Can I have you charge my phone at night? I just don't want the distraction in my room."

- If you have access to nudity on TV in your house, ask your parents to block that channel.

- If you think you might be addicted to porn, go to www.XXXChurch.com. They provide some great resources and information about how to free yourself from the slavery of porn.

25.

FOR ONE DAY, TRY REALLY HARD TO BE GOOD. THE NEXT DAY, GIVE UP AND LET JESUS CONTROL YOUR ACTIONS. WHICH ONE IS EASIER?

LOVE, JOY, PEACE. . .THESE ARE THE FRUIT OF THE Spirit, and we should try to model these attributes in our lives, right?

Wrong.

It's one of the most misinterpreted passages in the Bible. Sunday school teachers across America often teach the fruit of the Spirit in Galatians as a list of behaviors we should do. "Be loving. Have joy. Spread peace."

Wrong, wrong, wrong.

They missed the point.

The fact is, the fruit of the Spirit are attributes that appear in our lives when we give God control. We aren't supposed to try to bear fruit. . .fruit just happens when God is working through us. The only thing we do is give up and let God change us, making us more loving, more joyful, more peaceful. . .you get the idea.

If you have tried really hard to be good and failed over and over again, this is really good news! We aren't supposed to *try*. We're supposed to *give up*. More specifically, we're supposed to give up our lives to God.

Galatians 5:16 says it simply:

> Let the Holy Spirit guide your lives. Then you won't be doing what your sinful nature craves.

So how do we let the Holy Spirit guide our lives?

Think of it like driving a car. Maybe you're a really good driver. Maybe you're a NASCAR driver, one of the best. Guess what? Even those guys make mistakes. Even those guys get into wrecks, get speeding tickets, dent their bumpers every once in a while. No matter how good a driver you are. . .you're still going to mess up.

That's where your faith in God comes in. Your relationship with God begins when you say, "God, I can't drive anymore. You drive." Then you slide over into the passenger's seat and allow Him to take the wheel.

Open your Bible and read Galatians 5:16–26 and see what happens when you allow the Spirit to take control of your life.

FINAL THOUGHTS

Go ahead. Give it a shot. Try really hard to be good for just one day. Tomorrow, just give it up to God and say, "You drive." See which one is easier and which one is more effective.

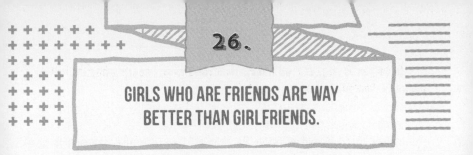

26.

GIRLS WHO ARE FRIENDS ARE WAY BETTER THAN GIRLFRIENDS.

WHAT'S THE DIFFERENCE BETWEEN A GIRLFRIEND AND a girl who is a friend?

I know, I know. . .it sounds like a stupid question. But honestly, think about the difference for a second. If most teenage guys were to describe a girlfriend, they would probably say something like this:

- Someone I'm attracted to
- Someone I can be romantic with, holding hands, kissing. . .
- Oh yeah. . .and someone I can talk with

If the same guys were to describe their best friends, they would probably say:

- Someone I can talk with
- Someone fun to hang out with
- Someone who will have my back if I need someone
- Someone who shares common interests

Lists may vary, but in many situations, guys are closer to their best friends who are girls than they are to their girlfriend. Girlfriends come and go, but best friends stick around.

Truthfully, guys often enter into relationships with girls primarily because of sexual attraction.

"Hey. What do you think about Kristy? She's gorgeous, she really seems to like you. . .but she's got nothing in common with you. . .*and she's an idiot.*"

"Sounds awesome!"

The relationship lasts as long as the romance is going well. But as soon as the first fight arises. . .the relationship typically ends.

The question I want to ask you is this: Who would you rather spend the rest of your life with?

Let me ask you another question: When you're married, how many hours or minutes each day will be dedicated to sex and romance? How many hours will that leave you to hang out with your friend with whom you've chosen to spend the rest of your life?

When looking for someone to spend the rest of your life with, I think most people would agree that the *friendship* part had better be pretty important. The perfect match would probably be a best friend who also happens to be attractive—and attracted—to you.

So why do we allow romance to trump friendship?

FINAL THOUGHTS

I encourage you to develop numerous friendships with girls as you go through your high school years. Look for girls with the following qualities:

- She shares the same love for God that you have
- You share common interests
- You enjoy doing activities together
- You can easily talk with her
- She's trustworthy

And if she happens to be attractive as well. . .that's a bonus! Build friendships with *that* kind of girl. . .and save the romance for later. The romance will happen when it's supposed to happen. Focus on the friendship.

27

DOING THE WRONG THING IS EASY, AND MOST PEOPLE DO IT. DOING THE RIGHT THING IS OFTEN DIFFICULT, AND FEW ACHIEVE IT. CHOOSE THE RIGHT PATH.

"JUSTIN GOT THE ANSWERS TO THE HISTORY TEST WE have to take after lunch. We made copies. Want one?"

"Did you see that new music video in the No. 1 spot on iTunes? There's naked girls in the preview! Wanna see?"

"Hey, everybody's getting together at Johnson's on Friday. His parents are going to be out of town—if you know what I mean. Are you going?"

In all these situations, yes is the easy answer. It's the answer most people would give. In fact, many teenagers today might make fun of you if you said no.

Let's be honest. It's hard to make the right decision when everyone else is making the wrong choice.

Maybe that's why Jesus said this:

> *"Enter through the narrow gate. For wide is the gate and broad is the road that leads to destruction, and many enter through it. But small is the gate and narrow the road that leads to life, and only a few find it."* (Matthew 7:13–14 NIV)

GO AHEAD, ANSWER. . .

+ What do you think Jesus is talking about here?

+ According to this verse, which road are most people using?

+ Where does this broad (wide) road lead?

+ Where does the narrow road lead?

+ Why do you think Jesus said that few people find the narrow road?

We encounter small decisions every day: the opportunity to cheat, to look at something inappropriate, or something as small as talking bad about someone we don't like. It's easy to say yes to these little temptations. Many do.

Do you want to be like everyone else?

Where does that road lead?

FINAL THOUGHTS

Living a life of faith in Jesus isn't easy. Jesus didn't go with the flow. He didn't conform to what everyone else was doing. He wasn't worried about popularity points.

Jesus did what was right!

Which road are you going to walk?

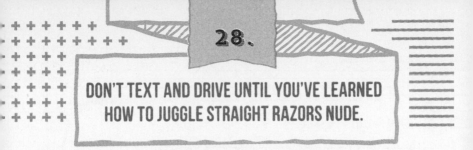

28.

DON'T TEXT AND DRIVE UNTIL YOU'VE LEARNED HOW TO JUGGLE STRAIGHT RAZORS NUDE.

"ONE QUICK LITTLE TEXT WON'T HURT."

That's what literally millions of teenage drivers say every year as they pull out their phone and fire off a quick text from behind the wheel.

That's what Savannah Nash thought when she attempted a quick text on her first solo drive after getting her driver's license. Less than a week after turning sixteen, Savannah got permission to go to the grocery store on an errand. She turned left while looking down at her phone, turning right into the path of a semitruck in oncoming traffic. She was killed instantly.[7]

According to a recent AT&T Teen Driver Survey of more than one thousand teenagers fifteen to nineteen years old. . .

- 97 percent of teens say texting while driving is "dangerous,"
- 75 percent claim it is "very dangerous," and
- 43 percent of these same teens still text and drive anyway.[8]

GO AHEAD, ANSWER. . .

+ Do you think most young people know that texting is dangerous?

+ Why do they still do it?

+ What do you think would help young people develop the discipline to ignore their phones while driving?

+ What would help you?

FINAL THOUGHTS

We know it's dangerous. . .yet we do it anyway.

Are you familiar with how sharp a straight razor is? I'm referring to those razors with a wide-open blade that barbers use.

Would you lie naked in a beanbag chair and attempt to juggle a few straight razors above your nether regions? Why not?

Why would you risk texting while piloting a couple thousand pounds of metal? The consequences could be far worse than even with the razors.

Next time you're tempted, remember one thing: *the text can wait.*

29

TAKE OFF YOUR HEADPHONES AND PLAY YOUR MUSIC OUT LOUD.

ACCORDING TO A RECENT MEDIA CONSUMPTION REPORT, kids between the ages of eight and eighteen spend more than two hours per day on average listening to music.[9] This number is only growing now that a majority of young people own smartphones and carry their entire music library everywhere they go.[10]

The question I want to propose to you is this: *Why headphones?*

I know not all music is played through headphones, but let's face it, a lot of teenagers like to wear their Beats by Dre earphones around the house, when they walk outside, or at their sporting events. Headphones are actually pretty popular.

I understand. I have a nice pair of noise-canceling headphones that I use on occasion.

What I'm talking about is when headphones become the primary speakers through which we listen to music. If it's not uncommon for your friends and family to see you walking around with headphones, here are a few things for you to consider:

- Headphones tell others, "I want to be alone."
- Headphones keep you from hearing what's going on around you.
- Headphones remove any accountability to what you're listening to (in other words, you can listen to raunchy music and nobody knows).

Don't get me wrong—there's nothing wrong with wanting some time to yourself every once in a while. But where's the line between "alone time" and just plain *antisocial*?

Music is an amazing connection point between people. Use music to connect with your friends and family. Most people have no problem playing music with their friends. . .but their family?

TRY THIS. . .

+ Get a docking station for your phone or iPod and use it as your primary music outlet.

+ Take the most recent song you downloaded and play it for your parents. Ask them what they think of it.

+ Ask them what their favorite music was when they were teenagers and listen to some of those songs with them.

+ Make a playlist for your parents, or for a family trip—something you can listen to together.

FINAL THOUGHTS

Music can be a lot of fun. Wouldn't it be nice if music helped you connect with your family instead of separating you from them?

Put the headphones aside. Let the music play out loud! (And if your parents complain, ask them to read this chapter.)

30

ALWAYS STOP AND TALK WITH THE HOMELESS.

THE HOMELESS ARE EASY TO IGNORE. . .WHICH IS what most people do.

Imagine their surprise if you actually stopped and talked with them.

I had a friend named Eric who passed homeless people on his way to work every day. He saw them standing with cardboard signs at his freeway exit each morning, and he often saw them near his grocery store. Some passersby handed these people money, but that made Eric wonder: *Are they just using the money for alcohol or drugs?*

Eric didn't like the fact that he used that as an excuse. It's easy to justify not getting involved. *I had better not give them money, because they'll just spend it on liquor!*

So why not give them food?

Giving food was much more difficult than money, but Eric was determined to help the needy people he saw each day. He started taking extra time each morning to make an additional lunch. Instead of making one sandwich for himself, he made two and packed the second one in an extra brown bag. Whatever Eric made for himself, he packed an extra one, as well. On his way to work, he'd give the extra lunch to a homeless person he saw along the way. This paved the way for some quick conversations each morning.

Eric's effort challenged me. I frequently see homeless people near my local grocery store. Most often they are asking for money, but I've never seen anyone turn down food.

I encounter so many needy people in my area that I now keep water bottles, granola bars, and McDonald's certificates in my car. Then I invite homeless people to a free meal at our church on the second Friday of every month.

Our church has been cooking meals for the needy for years now. Hundreds of families come out for Second Fridays, where they are fed, given clothes and blankets, and connected with the help they need. This gives us an opportunity to sit down at a table and have conversations with them. We ask simple questions like, "Where did you hear about Second Fridays?" "Where do you stay?" "Tell me your story."

We don't serve others for recognition or to fulfill community service hours; we do it because God wants us to serve others as if we were serving Him. As the apostle Paul says:

> *Serve wholeheartedly, as if you were serving the Lord, not people.* (Ephesians 6:7 NIV)

GO AHEAD, ANSWER. . .

+ What does it mean to serve wholeheartedly?

+ What would look like in your world?

+ Why should we serve as if we're serving the Lord, not people?

+ What does this tell us about what our attitudes should be?

FINAL THOUGHTS

Most homeless people didn't set out to become homeless. Somehow, one decision led to another, and they eventually found themselves barely scraping out a living each day.

It's not our job to judge them, but it is our job to reach out to them.

How can you help someone needy and strike up a conversation with them this week? Can you make an extra lunch tomorrow or buy some food certificates to give away? Make a plan to do something this week.

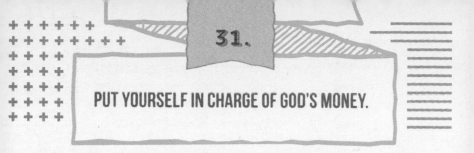

31.

PUT YOURSELF IN CHARGE OF GOD'S MONEY.

GOD DOESN'T WANT TO BE IN CHARGE OF OUR MONEY; He wants us to be in charge of His money. All of our money is His anyway. The question is, what are you going to do with God's money?

You can learn a lot about a person when you look at his spending. In Matthew 6:21, Jesus puts it like this:

> *"Wherever your treasure is, there the desires of your heart will also be."*

GO AHEAD, ANSWER. . .

+ According to the verse, where are the desires of your heart?

+ What does Jesus mean by this?

+ Why do you think Jesus said this?

I've met plenty of people who call themselves *believers* in Jesus. I'm one of them. I guess that's a good description of someone who has a relationship with Jesus, because Jesus wants us to put our complete trust in Him. If we truly *believe* in Him, it will be with our whole heart.

But does that also mean with our whole *wallets* as well?

Do we need to be reminded who put the money in our wallets in the first place?

God provides all we need. Many people forget that He is the provider as they begin storing up money and possessions, acquiring security from materialistic sources instead of from God.

Jesus warns us about this:

> And he told them this parable: "The ground of a certain rich man yielded an abundant harvest. He thought to himself, 'What shall I do? I have no place to store my crops.'

"Then he said, 'This is what I'll do. I will tear down my barns and build bigger ones, and there I will store my surplus grain. And I'll say to myself, "You have plenty of grain laid up for many years. Take life easy; eat, drink and be merry." '

"But God said to him, 'You fool! This very night your life will be demanded from you. Then who will get what you have prepared for yourself?'

"This is how it will be with whoever stores up things for themselves but is not rich toward God." (Luke 12:16–21 NIV)

Jesus was pretty clear when He talked about money—probably because He knew how easy it is to become greedy or to let money become our sense of security. We forget about God's provision and think, *If I get enough stuff, then everything will be okay.* How strong is our faith if our confidence is based on money?

God knows that the love of temporary riches can cause people to become distracted from an eternal relationship with Him. Maybe that's why He told a rich man to go sell everything he had and give it to the poor (Matthew 19:21).

Jesus wants us to put our trust in Him, not in our money. The best way to do that is to remember that it's not our money in the first place. It's all His.

How well are you managing His money?

FINAL THOUGHTS

The Christian life is a life of faith. This faith drives us to look beyond the temporary pleasures around us and fix our eyes on the eternal relationship with our Lord, Jesus Christ. This eternal focus helps us manage our money, because we realize it's not our money in the first place. It's His money. This makes it easier to give sacrificially and spend wisely. What are you going to do with God's money?

32

FIND A MENTOR.

DO YOU HAVE SOMEONE IN YOUR LIFE WHO MODELS how to live like Jesus?

Don't underestimate the power of a positive mentor.

The term *mentor* first emerged in *The Odyssey*, the classic Greek story in which King Odysseus calls on a trusted friend named Mentor to act as a guide and adviser to the king's young son, Telemachus, when Odysseus must leave for another country to fight a war.

Though mentoring has ancient roots, it isn't out of date by any means. In fact, over the past fifteen years, mentoring has been growing in popularity as an effective tool to help young people mature and make good decisions. Why? Because teachers, coaches, and youth workers everywhere have recognized how powerful and effective it can be when a caring adult takes time to invest in the life of someone younger.

Parents are always looking for positive ways to influence their kids' lives. That's probably why they always approach me after my parenting workshops and ask, "What is the one thing that makes the biggest difference in the lives of young people today?"

Any guesses on the answer?

I don't even have to think about it. The answer is practically undisputable: "A young man who has a positive adult role model in his life—someone who listens, encourages, and sometimes even advises—has the best chance for success in life."

Mentors make a huge difference.

In California alone, where I live, an estimated 2,300 mentoring programs are serving young people throughout the state. Research reveals that positive adult role models make a big difference in the lives of young people. In fact, in one survey, 72 percent of the respondents said they would actually be willing to pay more in taxes to fund mentoring programs.[11]

Mentoring is also biblical. Jesus modeled it with His disciples, devoting three years of His life to mentoring a group of twelve guys. When Jesus was crucified, eleven of those guys continued His ministry. The apostle Paul also became an effective mentor, and he gives us a blueprint for how to do it:

> *Follow my example, as I follow the example of Christ.*
> (1 Corinthians 11:1 NIV)

GO AHEAD, ANSWER. . .

+ Whose example did Paul instruct his readers to follow?

+ Whose example did Paul follow?

+ Why did he tell his readers to follow him, instead of just saying, "Follow Christ"?

Paul imitated Jesus and told others to imitate him as he imitated Jesus. In doing this, Paul gave them a visual representation of what following Jesus looked like.

Paul exemplified mentoring in his relationship with Timothy. Timothy didn't have a father, so Paul took on that role. He mentored Timothy and taught him how to follow Christ. As Paul followed Christ, Timothy followed Christ in Paul. This mentorship was so powerful that Paul was able to instruct the church in Corinth to imitate him by imitating Timothy.

> *Therefore I urge you to imitate me. For this reason I have sent to you Timothy, my son whom I love, who is faithful in the Lord. He will remind you of my way of life in Christ Jesus, which agrees with what I teach everywhere in every church.* (1 Corinthians 4:16–17 NIV)

FINAL THOUGHTS

Find a mentor. Ask someone you respect to meet with you weekly, or even monthly, to talk with you about real life and to coach you as you learn to walk in the ways of Jesus.

My daughter Ashley noticed the importance of mentorship and desired a mentoring relationship. Last year she decided that the only way to get a mentor was to ask someone. She approached my wife and me and asked, "Do you think Julie would be a good mentor?" Julie is a good friend of ours from our church—a great example of a follower of Christ.

"Julie would be an amazing mentor," we said.

Then Ashley asked Julie, "I'm looking for a mentor. Can we meet once or twice a month and just talk about real life?"

Julie gladly accepted and they began meeting. Now the two of them are reading through a Christian book together and meeting a couple of times a month.

Jesus modeled mentorship, Paul modeled mentorship . . . . I think mentorship is probably a pretty good model.

Whom can you contact this week and ask to mentor you?

33

WANNA BE AN INDIVIDUAL? POST SOME CONSTRUCTIVE AND AFFIRMING COMMENTS ONLINE.

HOW COME PEOPLE BECOME RUTHLESS IN THEIR COMMENTS about other people's pictures, posts, or videos?

I see it all the time. Someone posts a quick selfie or a video they shot with a friend. If the post gets any traffic. . .the comments start floating in: insults, expletives, crude remarks.

NBC's *Saturday Night Live* did a spoof about this phenomenon. They hosted a game show where they invited some of these mean commentators to guest star on the show. Then, without warning, they brought on some of the people whom they had insulted to confront them face-to-face. The results were hilarious as the mean commentators shrank in their chairs, embarrassed to be called out for their actions.

The skit shed light on the crux of the problem: *anonymity*.

Commentators are often anonymous. Who really knows who JDog2489 is? Maybe that's why JDog2489 is such a coward, cutting everyone down in the comments section.

God calls us to be a light in a dark world. In fact, Jesus specifically says,

> *"Let your light shine before others, that they may see your good deeds and glorify your Father in heaven."* (Matthew 5:16 NIV)

GO AHEAD, ANSWER. . .

+ How can we let our light shine before others?

+ What might this look like in the context of social media?

+ Why does this verse say we should let our light shine before others?

+ According to the verse, when others see our good deeds, whom will they glorify?

+ How could your good deeds cause someone else to praise God?

The Internet is full of mean people. Wanna be an individual? Post something constructive and affirming in your online comments. I know it can be difficult. Sometimes people post some really lame stuff that is just begging to be made fun of. And most people take the bait. Show them you're different.

FINAL THOUGHTS

We have the opportunity to reflect God in our lives by how we treat others.

Think about the people who encountered you today. What would they say about you? What would they say about God if they found out you were one of His followers?

How can you let your light shine for God in your world this week, both cyber and real?

34.

OPEN DOORS FOR ALL WOMEN AND GIRLS. . .ALWAYS!

IT'S THE SIMPLEST HABIT YOU'LL EVER LEARN, BUT IT reveals to everyone what you think about women.

It's like this: You and your mom are walking toward the door of the local mall. As you approach the door, even if she's ahead of you, take a couple of quick steps, get to the door first, and open it for her.

That's it.

It doesn't matter who it is: your grandma, your sister, your mom. . .a total stranger! Always open the door for women and girls.

When you open a door, it sends a positive message:

- I respect women.
- I am mannerly and chivalrous.
- Women deserve men who put women first.
- I am a servant who is not afraid to humble myself.
- Momma didn't raise no dummy!

This one simple act communicates that you value women, and they'll respect you for it.

FINAL THOUGHTS

It doesn't matter if it's a car door, the door to your house, the door to a store. . .open doors for women and girls and show them there are still some men who know how to treat them right.

35.

GRAB A FRIEND AND GO VOLUNTEER SOMEWHERE.

YOUNG PEOPLE TODAY GET A LOT OF CRITICISM.

"You guys are always staring at your phones!"

"You only care about yourselves!"

"You're the most inconsiderate generation!"

I've heard it all. But I think adults sometimes overlook one of the undeniable characteristics about the millennial generation: *you care.*

It's true. We can't deny that your generation cares. You volunteer at a higher rate than preceding generations. You buy shoes from companies that give shoes away to the needy. And when you graduate and move into the workplace, you choose companies that provide volunteer opportunities.

No one understands exactly why, but your generation wants to make an impact.

I don't think some young people understand the potential impact they could make. You have the power to make a huge difference in the lives of others. Give it a try. Grab a friend and go volunteer somewhere. Visit a nursing home. Work at a homeless shelter. Ask your church office how you can help.

Volunteering is the most fun when you're able to use your skills doing something you're good at.

GO AHEAD, ANSWER. . .

+ Where is a place near you where you could volunteer?

+ What kind of causes do you like to support, and what kind of needs do you like to meet?

+ What abilities or skills do you have that could help others?

+ How could these skills help others?

+ Sometime in the next month, when could you make time to volunteer?

Chances are, there is a church, mission, or organization near you that could really use your help. Maybe they want to use social media to reach out to the community but don't know how. Maybe they need someone to work in their office. Maybe they need someone to mow their lawn.

You may never know unless you ask.

FINAL THOUGHTS

You can make a difference. Grab a friend and go volunteer somewhere near you. You'll make new friends—and better yet, you'll make an impact.

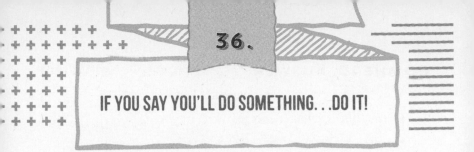

36

IF YOU SAY YOU'LL DO SOMETHING...DO IT!

"I'LL BE THERE."

Will he really show up? He's said it many times before, but usually "something comes up" and he cancels. So now, if you're being realistic, you know there's about a 50 percent chance that he will actually show up.

Is that how you want to be perceived? As the guy who only *sometimes* means what he says?

It happens all the time. People say something, but they really don't mean it. Maybe it's the way they were raised. Maybe in their house they were taught that yes means *maybe*.

"I really need your help on Saturday. I have an opportunity to do some yard work for my neighbor, but he needs two people. Can I count on you?"

"Yep. I'll be there."

"Perfect. I won't ask anyone else. See ya Saturday."

Saturday comes, and you get a text thirty minutes beforehand.

SORRY DUDE. . .I WAS OUT LATE LAST NIGHT AND I HAVE A LOT OF HOMEWORK TODAY.

Now you're stuck doing a two-man job by yourself. In addition, your neighbor is mad because you told him you'd have a friend helping you. Now he has to come out and help you lift a few things because you can't do it by yourself. That means he had to cancel his plans that day.

All because someone's "yes" didn't mean yes.

We need to be people who keep our word and mean it when we say yes (Matthew 5:37).

In Psalm 15, the author describes a person who has a relationship with God. He describes this person as blameless, righteous, and speaking "truth from their heart." But then he goes on to list a quality that few people have—someone "who keeps an oath even when it hurts, and does not change their mind" (Psalm 2, 4 NIV).

GO AHEAD, ANSWER. . .

+ What does it mean to keep an oath or keep your word?

+ Why is it important to keep your word?

+ What does he mean "even when it hurts"?

+ Why does the psalmist say, "even when it hurts"?

+ Describe a time when you told someone yes but then circumstances changed.

+ Would it have "hurt" to keep your commitment?

The world is full of flaky people. Sadly, *yes* doesn't always mean yes anymore. What if you were different? What if you were a person people could count on?

FINAL THOUGHTS

If you say you'll do something, do it. If you say you'll be there, show up. Very few people have someone they can truly count on. You can be that person.

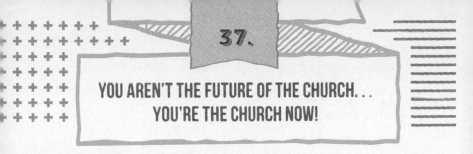

YOU AREN'T THE FUTURE OF THE CHURCH. . .
YOU'RE THE CHURCH NOW!

THE PASTOR STEPPED TO THE PULPIT AND LOOKED down at the young people seated in the audience. "I'm so glad to see all you young people here. You are the future of the church!"

I hate it when people say that.

Please don't misunderstand. It's not that what the pastor said is wrong, but I can't help but wonder if his words breed a certain passivity among teenagers. When you hear the word, I'm afraid you might think, *I'll be something worthwhile* later. *Meanwhile, I'm really not important. I'm like a caterpillar in a cocoon or a piece of bread in the toaster. . . .*

The fact is, young people are the church *right now*. In fact, young people can do what many others can't do.

- You have better access to reach out to other young people.
- You volunteer at higher rates than older generations.
- You are better at multitasking than older generations.
- You are more technically savvy than older generations.
- You have the power and capacity to make a difference *now*.

In addressing a similar issue, Paul writes to Timothy:

> *Don't let anyone think less of you because you are young.*
> *Be an example to all believers in what you say, in the way*
> *you live, in your love, your faith, and your purity.* (1 Timothy
> 4:12)

GO AHEAD, ANSWER. . .

+ What does the verse say we shouldn't let anyone do?

+ Why do you think Paul told Timothy this?

+ What are the ways that Paul affirmed Timothy to be an example?

+ How can we be examples to all believers in what we say?

+ How can we be an example in the way we live?

+ How can we be an example in our love?

+ How can we be an example in our faith?

+ How can we be an example in our purity?

It's as if Paul is telling Timothy, "Right now, you are supposed to be the example of all these things. You are to be the example of Christianity." That's a huge responsibility. . .and he gave it to a young person.

FINAL THOUGHTS

Don't be fooled into thinking you're just some useless kid hanging around church. You are so much more than that. You have the potential, and the opportunity, to be an example of Christ to your friends, your family, and people in your community. Yes, you are the future of the church, but you are also the *present* church.

How are you going to live up to that responsibility?

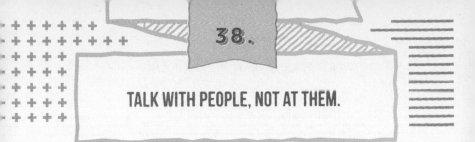

TALK WITH PEOPLE, NOT AT THEM.

WHAT IS THE DIFFERENCE BETWEEN A DIALOGUE AND a monologue? Which do you prefer?

Dialogue is when two people interact with each other. One person talks a little while the other listens, and then they reverse roles. Both people get a chance to share, and both feel heard.

Monologue is when one person talks and the other person just sits and listens. How fun is that?

GO AHEAD, ANSWER. . .

Think about the conversations between. . .

+ you and your parents. *Dialogue or monologue?*

+ you and your teachers. *Dialogue or monologue?*

+ you and your friends at school. *Dialogue or monologue?*

+ you and your best friend. *Dialogue or monologue?*

+ you and your siblings. *Dialogue or monologue?*

Now go back and circle the person who usually does the most talking in each of the examples above.

Think of the last time you felt truly heard. Remember how nice it was when someone listened to how you felt and acknowledged what you said?

Sometimes the best gift we can give someone is a listening ear.

- Ask questions about something they want to talk about. ("You have a lot of hockey gear. Do you play? Where is hockey in your future?")
- Look people in the eye as they talk.
- Ask clarifying questions about the way they felt. ("It sounds like that made you feel cheated.")
- Don't turn the conversation back to yourself. ("Oh, you went camping? I always go camping. I like to. . .I. . .I. . .I. . .")

And do you want some good dating advice? Girls love a guy who is a good listener.

FINAL THOUGHTS

If you have a tendency to monopolize conversations, turn your monologues into dialogues. Listen; don't lecture. Talk *with* people, not *at* them.

DON'T GET CAUGHT UP IN THE PRESENT.

"YOU'RE LIVING FOR THE INCH."

That's what my friend Greg Stier would say. Do you have a twenty-five-foot tape measure? Pull out an inch and take a peek. Let's say that inch represents one hundred years. That would be a long time to live, right?

Now pull out all twenty-five feet. That would be thirty thousand years. Can you imagine living that long?

Let's just say you could keep pulling out that measuring tape and wrapping it around the earth—not just once, but again and again—until finally the whole planet was covered with yellow measuring tape. That would be a long time. . . right?

That's only the first day of eternity.

It's easy to get distracted by "the inch." Think about it. We are so preoccupied with school, friends, family, girlfriends. . .that we forget to live a life of faith, knowing there is life beyond the inch.

And that's what it really comes down to: *faith.* We use the word *faith* all the time. "My faith in Jesus." "My life of faith." But what would it be like to live a true life of faith, where we believe there is much more to this world than just the temporary stuff we see all around us?

Hebrews 11:1 defines faith in a way that looks beyond the inch:

> *Faith is the confidence that what we hope for will actually happen; it gives us assurance about things we cannot see.*

Sometimes we get distracted by temporary pleasures. Other times we grow fatigued with struggles. That's where faith comes in. The drama, struggles, and trials you're experiencing are only temporary and are shaping you to be the man you're becoming! Don't get caught up in the present. Learn to live with an *eternal focus.*

Imagine living a life of faith, knowing there is life beyond the inch. Here's what that might look like:

- Consistently read your Bible, or studies like the ones in this book, reminding yourself daily of life beyond the inch.
- Pray continually, asking God to help you live a life of faith, living for eternity.
- When temptations come your way, remind yourself that temporary distractions will only hurt your eternal relationship with God (1 Peter 2:11).
- When tough situations arise, remember this: "Our present sufferings are not worth comparing with the glory that will be revealed in us" (Romans 8:18 NIV).

FINAL THOUGHTS

Many people will live their entire lives grasping at temporary fixes to a permanent problem. God wants a relationship with us, a relationship that lasts far beyond the inch. When we put our trust in Jesus, we begin a relationship that no one can ever take away from us. This gives us the assurance to live a life of faith, to live beyond the present, with the joy that this life offers, which is so much more than what we see around us.

Do you have this kind of relationship with Jesus?

Pray right now and tell Him that you want to put your trust in Him and live "life beyond the inch."

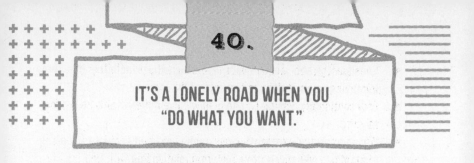

40.

IT'S A LONELY ROAD WHEN YOU "DO WHAT YOU WANT."

IN THE SUMMER OF 2013, MILEY CYRUS CAME OUT with a song with the following lyrics:

> It's our party we can do what we want
> It's our party we can say what we want
> It's our party we can love who we want[12]

Repeated throughout the chorus is the line:

> Doing whatever we want

Wouldn't that be nice? I guess it's possible. . .as long as you don't care about consequences.

Let me explain.

Miley's philosophy doesn't work, because it's selfish and someone always ends up paying the price. Think about it. If you do whatever *you* want, then *someone else* doesn't get to do what *he* or *she* wants.

Let's say you and your friend Jeff are both staring at the last piece of cake, and you both want it. Miley's song assures you both that you can do what you want. So Jeff says, "I can do whatever I want" and eats the entire piece of cake. Now you're mad, because you didn't get what you wanted.

Taking Miley's advice to the next level, you decide you're going to *say* whatever you want. "Jeff, I hate you."

Jeff doesn't like this, even though it's what *you* wanted to say at the moment. But that's okay, because Jeff has been eyeing your girlfriend. After all, she's gorgeous, and Miley says you can love whomever you want. Jeff and your girlfriend both believe Miley, so they start making out.

Everyone is just doing what Miley said—"Doing whatever we want"—and nobody's happy.

You all get in a big fight, Jeff makes an off-color remark about your girlfriend (after all, he can say what he wants, right?), and then she slaps Jeff and all three of you walk away hurt and upset. . .and *you're* still hungry for cake!

What the heck happened here? Maybe Miley's philosophy is a little short-sighted.

The Bible offers something a little less popular but 100 percent true. It's up to you to decide which philosophy to follow: popular. . .or true?

In an earlier chapter, we looked at Galatians 5. Let's take a closer look at two of those verses:

> *Let the Holy Spirit guide your lives. Then you won't be doing what your sinful nature craves. The sinful nature wants to do evil, which is just the opposite of what the Spirit wants. And the Spirit gives us desires that are the opposite of what the sinful nature desires.* (Galatians 5:16–17)

Compare that wisdom to Miley's "do what we want, say what we want, love who we want" mantra.

Imagine going through life doing exactly what you feel like doing at any moment, saying whatever you want, loving whomever you feel like loving at that moment, kissing whomever you want (even if it's not the person you love at the moment—after all, you can do whatever you want). I think you get the idea.

GO AHEAD, ANSWER. . .

+ What are some consequences you might face if you do whatever you want?

+ What are some consequences you might experience if you say whatever you want?

+ What would be the result of kissing whomever you want?

+ What happens when people live however they want?

+ What does Paul offer in Galatians as an alternative way to live?

If we live selfish lives, we will live lonely lives. No one wants to be around people who do whatever they want.

FINAL THOUGHTS

Miley's song isn't the first ever to talk about doing "whatever feels good" at the moment. Sadly, this philosophy just doesn't work. It's selfish, it hurts others, and it eventually hurts us.

God offers us so much more when we depend on His Spirit to guide our lives. Paul shows us what our lives will produce when we let the Holy Spirit control us:

> The Holy Spirit produces this kind of fruit in our lives: love, joy, peace, patience, kindness, goodness, faithfulness, gentleness, and self-control. There is no law against these things! (Galatians 5:22–23)

It's really up to you. You can take the selfish and lonely path, which leads to hurt all around, or you can take the Spirit-led path, allowing God to control your thinking, which results in love, joy, peace, and all those good things. Which end result sounds better to you?

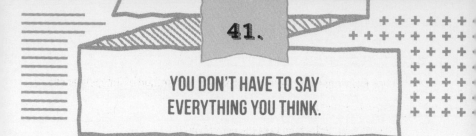

41.

YOU DON'T HAVE TO SAY EVERYTHING YOU THINK.

MR. ROBERTSON LEANED BACK IN HIS CHAIR. HE HAD been the school counselor for more than twenty years. He loved talking to students about their future. "It's good that you're signing up for US History next year," he told Baily. "You never know when you're gonna have to know that George Washington, Benjamin Franklin, and John Adams were three of the main authors of the Declaration of Independence."

Baily had just visited Philadelphia and had studied about the Declaration of Independence. "George Washington wasn't one of the authors," she said, smiling. "I think you mean Thomas Jefferson."

Mr. Robertson's forehead wrinkled. "No, it was George Washington."

Baily tapped a couple of keys on her phone, doing a quick Internet search. She quickly found what she was looking for. She turned the screen around and showed Mr. Robertson the following:

> *Although Thomas Jefferson is often called the "author" of the Declaration of Independence, he wasn't the only person who contributed important ideas. Jefferson was a member of a five-person committee appointed by the Continental Congress to write the Declaration. The committee included Jefferson, Benjamin Franklin, John Adams, Robert Livingston, and Roger Sherman.*

Mr. Robertson leaned forward and read the screen. When he finished he leaned back in his chair. "Hmmmm. I guess I was thinking of the Constitution."

He shuffled a couple of pages on his desk. "Well, I have some other appointments I must attend to." He looked up at Baily, a little detached. "Any other questions?"

When Baily left the office she felt terrible.

She had won. She was right.

But she definitely lost out in this situation.

GO AHEAD, ANSWER. . .

+ Was Baily right with her facts about the Declaration of Independence?

+ Why did Baily feel bad?

+ How did Mr. Robertson take the correction?

+ What should Baily have done in this situation?

Just because we're right doesn't mean we have to *prove* we're right. Some battles are worth fighting, and some are better to walk away from.

Proverbs 13:3 offers some pretty wise advice:

Those who control their tongue will have a long life;
opening your mouth can ruin everything.

+ When was a recent time when you should have held your tongue but didn't?

+ How could you have handled the situation differently?

+ What does Proverbs say will happen with those who control their tongues?

+ Why will people who hold their tongues have a long life?

FINAL THOUGHTS

The tongue is a powerful weapon. We can use it to lift people up or to tear others down.

Which would you like to be known for?

42.

LIVE LIFE WITH THE KNOWLEDGE THAT YOU ARE BEING WATCHED AND IMITATED.

I ALWAYS LOVED MY COUSIN RANDY, WHO IS SEVERAL years older than I am. He was always fun, adventurous. . .and just a little crazy!

I remember when I was five and Randy was nine. We were at a camp with our families, and a bunch of big high school kids took over the swimming pool. One kid thought he was really cool and floated out in the middle of the pool on a tube, fully dressed, and sipping a Pepsi.

Randy turned to us and whispered, "Watch this."

The high school kids didn't even notice the little nine-year-old jump off the diving board and disappear to the bottom of the pool. Seconds later, Randy surfaced like a breaching whale, easily toppling the teenager into the water. The crowd laughed hysterically.

Randy was the coolest. He took us on motorcycle and snowmobile rides, and when he finally got his driver's license, he took us to concerts and on other fun escapades.

Children always look up to older kids. It doesn't take much. There's something about an older brother, cousin, or friend.

Whether you like it or not, you are being watched. It may be at church, school, or a family reunion. If you have little brothers or sisters, it's happening in your home. Those younger kids are watching you and using you as a model for how to behave. They are noting your attitude, your language, and even your demeanor. They'll repeat phrases you barely remember saying.

You are a role model.

With this honor comes great responsibility.

In Matthew 18:5–7, Jesus talks to us about the importance of our impact on young'uns:

> *"Anyone who welcomes a little child like this on my behalf is welcoming me. But if you cause one of these little ones who trusts in me to fall into sin, it would be better for you to have a large millstone tied around your neck and be*

drowned in the depths of the sea. What sorrow awaits the
world, because it tempts people to sin. Temptations are
inevitable, but what sorrow awaits the person who does the
tempting."

GO AHEAD, ANSWER. . .

+ How could someone cause a little one to fall into sin?

+ What does Jesus say about this person?

+ What are some common behaviors that younger kids notice from older kids?

+ How much do you think young people copy their role models?

+ What are some things you have done that might have been copied by young people around you?

FINAL THOUGHTS

Live life with the knowledge that you are being watched and imitated. Younger kids will always look up to you just because you're older, and you can make a huge impact on them. . .negative or positive. I recommend choosing the positive.

43.

THAT SIN NO ONE KNOWS ABOUT? IT'S TIME TO TELL SOMEONE.

CARRIE WAS A SENIOR IN HIGH SCHOOL AND WAS respected by all her friends. She was a student leader at her church and led a midweek Bible study. That's why everyone was shocked when she said it.

"I've got some junk in my life that I need to confess."

That was the exact word she used: *junk*.

It was the last night of camp, and people were sharing about how God had impacted them that week at camp. Carrie took the microphone and began to share. After that opening line, she expanded a little about what she meant.

"A year ago when I sat here at this camp, I had that same junk in my life. So I sat down with Cindy back then and asked her to pray for me."

Everyone at the camp knew Cindy. She was one of the adult volunteers who was a cabin counselor every year, and the teenagers all loved her. They knew they could always trust her and talk with her.

Carrie went on. "Cindy asked me, 'What is it?'

"I told Cindy, 'I'd rather not say. It's just some junk that doesn't belong in my life. Will you pray for me?' Cindy and I prayed right then and there."

Carrie continued, "A year passed, but the junk didn't go away. I've struggled with it for the last year."

Carrie looked around at all the teenagers in the room. "Last night I couldn't stand it anymore, so I pulled Cindy aside and told her, 'Remember that junk I said I had in my life? It's still there.'

"Cindy told me, 'Carrie, if you tell me what it is, maybe we can work on it together.'

"So I did. I shared every little detail with her. I dumped it all on Cindy. We cried, we prayed. . .and then something happened."

As everyone listened to Carrie's words, the room was silent. "I felt this huge burden lift off my shoulders. I hadn't felt that free in a year. I was finally free from the secret I had been carrying around. And Cindy and I made a plan of how to deal with—with this junk!"

Then Carrie leaned in really close to the microphone and said something I'll never forget. "If you have some junk in your life right now. . .I don't care what it is. Verbalize it to someone. Because If you can't verbalize it, then you will never deal with it."

With that, Carrie sat down. That night almost a hundred kids began talking with their counselors about "junk" they needed to deal with. I've never seen so much honesty and so much confession at an evening campfire. All because one girl showed them the freedom that confession and accountability provide.

James 5:16 gives us some pretty good advice:

> Confess your sins to each other and pray for each other so
> that you may be healed. The earnest prayer of a righteous
> person has great power and produces wonderful results.

Maybe you're carrying around some "junk" in your life that you need to deal with. It might be embarrassing, and it might require some serious changes in your life. But down deep you want freedom from the burden you've been carrying around with you. The only freedom from that burden is through Jesus. Jesus is willing to take that burden from you. Consider doing what Carrie recommended, and what James recommends in his letter in the Bible. *Verbalize* it to someone else.

GO AHEAD, ANSWER. . .

+ Why do you think confessing our sins to others is helpful?

+ Why do you think Carrie said, "If you can't verbalize it, then you will never deal with it"?

+ Why is it nice to have someone who knows about our weaknesses?

+ What kind of help and accountability can a friend or loved one provide?

+ What is a sin you might need to confess today?

+ Who can you confess it to?

FINAL THOUGHTS

I leave you with the wise advice of a teenage girl: "If you have some junk in your life right now. . .I don't care what it is. Verbalize it. Verbalize it to someone. Because if you can't verbalize it, then you will never deal with it."

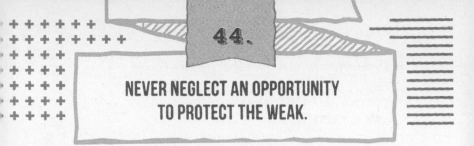

44.

NEVER NEGLECT AN OPPORTUNITY
TO PROTECT THE WEAK.

WHEN I WAS SEVENTEEN YEARS OLD, I WAS HANGING out at the lake with my friends. We had just gone to the snack bar and I had bought a tray of nachos. I remember they had the perfect amount of cheese (the girl at the snack bar wasn't stingy).

As we were walking back to our beach chairs, we heard some raised voices. Three drunk guys, who were easily in their twenties, had gathered around a young high school kid and were yelling at him. I don't know what happened or whose fault it was. All I saw was one small kid about to be beaten up by three large intoxicated men!

I handed my nachos to my friend Troy and stepped next to the guy in the middle, now surrounded by the three provokers.

I can't remember my exact words, but I said something like, "I don't know what happened here, but three-on-one is never fair."

More words were exchanged, and a couple more high school guys stepped into the middle to join us. Soon, the inebriated attackers walked away.

It's probably the only slightly heroic moment in my life. Unfortunately, no girls gave me a kiss afterward, and I don't even remember if the young kid in the middle said thanks. I do remember getting my nachos back from my friend, though, and enjoying them thoroughly.

Looking back, I'm not completely sure why I did it. Probably because I had been that guy in the middle plenty of times. When I was in elementary school, I had some of the biggest buckteeth you'd ever seen. My two front teeth stuck out further than humanly possible. I grew up hearing every name in the book: Bugs Bunny, Bucky Beaver, Can Opener (yeah, that was a clever one). . .you name it. I was often the victim of teasing and bullying.

I knew what it was like to be the guy getting punk'd by everyone around him.

Every once in a while, someone would stick up for me. Sometimes a simple "Hey, leave him alone" was enough. I even had a few people step in and say, "This is my friend."

I can't even express how good it felt when someone defended me.

When you defend someone, you express the heart of God:

He feels pity for the weak and the needy, and he will rescue them. (Psalm 72:13)

I could show you countless other verses throughout the Bible that speak of God's compassionate heart. He constantly reminds us to take care of the weak, the widows, and the orphans. Jesus, in one of His most famous sermons, the Sermon on the Mount, asks us to mourn for others, be merciful, and even go as far as allowing ourselves to be persecuted for doing what is right (Matthew 5:3–10).

GO AHEAD, ANSWER. . .

+ Describe a time when you saw someone being bullied, teased, or picked on.

+ How did you respond?

+ How should you have responded?

FINAL THOUGHTS

The world is full of bullies who prey on the weak and the hurting. You can make an incredible difference in people's lives by standing up for them when they are being mistreated. Never neglect an opportunity to protect the weak.

45.

DO YOU WANT TO ATTRACT GIRLS?
BRUSH YOUR TEETH!

COFFEE, ONIONS, GARLIC. . .ALL BREATH KILLERS.

It's a common fact, but many guys miss it. They walk up to a girl and start talking, clueless to the fact that their breath is an assault weapon.

The solution is simple: brush your teeth and get rid of that funk!

Sometimes a simple toothbrushing won't work. If you struggle with bad breath, consider the following:

- Avoid foods like onions and garlic, and drinks like coffee.
- Brush your teeth after every meal. Use a toothpaste that fights bad breath. Brush your tongue and the roof of your mouth.
- Floss nightly (which will prevent scraps of food hiding in your gums and turning into something nasty).
- Carry breath mints or gum.

Don't obsess about bad breath, but at the same time, pay respect to the people around you by taking care of your oral hygiene.

FINAL THOUGHTS

Your family, your friends. . .and the girl you like. . .will all appreciate it if you make an effort to have clean breath.

46

TALK TO HER FACE-TO-FACE.

HEY GIRL, WHASSUP?

NOTHIN' MUCH.

MISSIN' YOU.

I MISS YOU.

I WANT TO SPEND MORE TIME WITH YOU.

ME, TOO.

I THINK I LOVE YOU.

WOW. THAT WOULD HAVE BEEN REALLY COOL. . .IF YOU WOULD HAVE SAID IT TO MY FACE.

Texting and messaging has become so common that people now have some of their deepest conversations via messaging.

WILL U MARRY ME?

Lame.

We've even seen some celebrities take the easy way out of a relationship, using a text message to do their dirty work:

I WANT A DIVORCE.

I'm not knocking digital communication. I use it all the time with my own kids, and I sometimes prefer it for quick reminders. But it's sad when texting and other types of messaging begin to replace face-to-face communication to the extent that people become uncomfortable looking another person in the eye and talking.

I've noticed this trend in the last decade. Teenagers get in the same room with each other and they still retreat to their phones. I've seen two teenagers sitting on the same couch texting each other—not because it was fun, not because they didn't want others to hear, but simply because it was easier. These two didn't know how to talk face-to-face.

A real man knows how to talk to a woman face-to-face.

Don't get me wrong. I'm not down on technology, but I am willing to admit its shortfalls. Texting lacks nonverbal cues. In other words, you can't see when a person is smiling or hear when he or she is sarcastic or angry. That's why we've developed emoticons, to try to replace nonverbal cues. Like when we type: I HATE YOU. J

What the heck does that mean? Does she really hate me, and is trying to lessen the blow with that stupid smiley emoticon, or is she slightly passive-aggressive? Maybe it's neither, and she's totally kidding. But it's hard to tell when someone isn't right in front of you.

My seventeen-year-old daughter recently confessed, "I don't do any serious communication on my phone anymore. It always leads to fights." She shared an example of miscommunication in her conversations with a guy she liked. They were trying to have a deep conversation through texts. "It didn't work," she said. "I couldn't tell when he was serious or when he was being sarcastic. Finally, I just told him, 'Let's just talk about this tomorrow face-to-face.'"

Not bad advice. Actually, it's very wise advice.

The more teenagers I talk with about the subject, the more I hear the same thing: "It's not smart to have deep conversations via text message."

FINAL THOUGHTS

Man up. Look her in the eye and say it to her face.

Texting isn't bad; it's actually quite handy. But don't let it replace face-to-face conversation. Girls will appreciate a guy who can look them in the eye, listen (a lot), and talk (a little) without retreating to his phone.

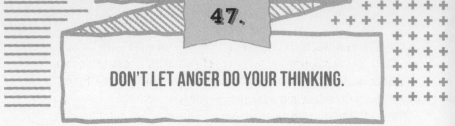

47.

DON'T LET ANGER DO YOUR THINKING.

NEVER MAKE IMPORTANT DECISIONS WHEN YOU'RE tired, scared, or emotional in any way. And absolutely never when you're angry. You don't want your anger to speak for you.

In 1962 an unusual superhero arrived on the comic book scene. The Incredible Hulk possessed unbelievable strength that actually grew stronger the angrier he became.

When I was a kid in the 1980s, the Hulk found a spot on a weekly TV show. Week after week, we watched a man named David Banner get bullied or hurt, being pushed to the point of anger. Then his muscles would start to bulge, his clothes would rip, his skin would turn green, and Banner would transform into anger incarnate—the Incredible Hulk.

After the Hulk finished his butt-kicking rampage, usually of people who deserved it, he would calm down, his muscles would shrink, and he would morph back into the mere human form of David Banner. Banner would then walk around and try to figure out what kind of damage he'd done as the Hulk. He would eventually move from that city, wandering to the next town, where he'd get beat up and become angry again.

The story of the Hulk is an interesting glimpse into the world of anger. The Hulk was David Banner's alter ego, with separate thoughts and (certainly) separate ways of handling situations. This isn't far from reality. When we become angry, we often act completely different than we would while calm. We say things we don't mean and make decisions we regret.

That's why it's best not to make important decisions while angry. Don't tell someone how you feel about them when you're angry, because it might not be *you* talking. Don't break up with your girlfriend when you're angry. Don't quit the basketball team when the coach ticks you off.

When I was in high school, I got angry at my brother and put my fist through a wall.

Do you know how expensive it is to pay a guy to come out and repair Sheet-rock, and then texture and paint a wall? A lot more than a high school kid wants to pay, I'll tell you that.

Once, in a fit of anger, I yelled at one of my friends, "I can't stand you. I've never liked you. You just follow me around every day and I put up with you."

Whoops! Our friendship was never the same after that.

Don't let your anger do your thinking.

In Paul's letter to the Galatians, he lists a bunch of sins to avoid, including idolatry, sorcery, jealousy, and "outbursts of anger" (Galatians 5:20).

GO AHEAD, ANSWER. . .

+ Why do you think "outbursts of anger" is included on this list?

+ Is anger in itself wrong?

+ Describe the difference between feeling angry and an "outburst of anger."

+ Why are "outbursts of anger" wrong?

Anger isn't wrong; but when we let anger do our thinking and we spit out whatever comes to mind during an angry moment. . .damage usually occurs.

When you're angry, walk away and give it some time. Don't allow yourself to spout off something stupid that you'll regret, and don't make any decisions in the moment that you'll regret later.

FINAL THOUGHTS

The Hulk is a fictional superhero. Yes, he somehow found a way to help people out when he was angry. If only that worked for us. Newsflash: you ain't ripped and you ain't green, and your angry outbursts never help anyone.

Never do or decide anything in anger. Anger isn't always bad, but you don't want to be controlled by it. Give it some time. Get a clear head. Walk away if you have to, and decide later. Never let anger do your thinking.

48

IF YOU WANT TO BE A BETTER MAN,
BE A BETTER DISCIPLE OF JESUS.

DESCRIBE JESUS.

Seriously. List His characteristics:

- Humble
- Wise
- Great leader
- Incredible teacher
- Cared for the poor and sick
- Talked with people no one else would talk with
- Loved children
- Servant leader
- Self-controlled

The list goes on.

How would you like to have some of those qualities?

It's simple. If you want to be a better man, be a better disciple of Jesus.

Jesus was everything a man should be. He was strong but meek. He was committed but forgiving of those who weren't. He was loving but didn't allow others to be taken advantage of.

Jesus was also a remarkable leader. He discipled twelve guys who almost all died a martyr's death for His cause. Now His followers number in the millions.

But how did He lead? He exemplified leadership by living out the principle of the first shall be last, by washing feet, and by eventually laying down His life for us.

If you want to be a true man, follow Jesus' example.

Jesus' invitation to His followers was simple:

> *"Follow Me, and I will make you become fishers of men."*
> (Mark 1:17 NASB)

Jesus asks us to do two things:

1. *Follow me.* Becoming a disciple of Jesus begins when we stop whatever we're doing and begin following Him. This is often referred to as "repentance" in the Bible (Acts 3:19). This means we stop going our own way and go His way instead.

2. *Allow me to make you.* Once we decide to follow Jesus, He will gradually transform us to be more like Him (Romans 12:1–2).

FINAL THOUGHTS

Do you want to be a man who loves others, cares for the weak, stands up for what is right, and forgives others when they are wrong?

Well, that's what women want. And they'll find that in Jesus.

If you want to be a better man, be a better disciple of Jesus.

49.

MAKE FRIENDS WITH SOMEONE WHO INSPIRES YOU TO DO WHAT'S RIGHT.

LET'S FACE IT. SOME FRIENDS SEEM TO INSPIRE GOOD in us, and some tend to drag us toward. . .something not so good.

Who are you spending the most time with?

Finish the sentence:

- If I ever get into trouble at school with a friend, it's most likely going to be with. . .
- If I ever sneak and do something I shouldn't with a friend, it's most likely going to be with. . .
- If I'm ever inspired by a friend to do something good, I'm usually inspired by. . .
- I find that I make wiser decisions when I hang out with. . .

It's nice when our friends inspire us to do good.

I'm not saying you should "unfriend" someone who is a troublemaker. You can still love this person and try to be someone who inspires him or her to be good. But who are the people you surround yourself with? Who are the people who inspire you the most?

Proverbs 27:17 NIV offers us some really great advice:

As iron sharpens iron, so one person sharpens another.

GO AHEAD, ANSWER. . .

+ What does Proverbs 27:17 mean?

+ How can one person sharpen another?

+ Who sharpens you?

+ Whom do you sharpen?

God loves relationships. He created us to be in a relationship with Him and also to enjoy relationships with others. Most of the Bible is about our relationships with God and others.

We can choose good friends or lousy friends. It's our choice. God wants us to surround ourselves with people who will sharpen us.

Make friends with someone who inspires you to do what's right.

FINAL THOUGHTS

Who truly sharpens you to be a better man of God? Call or text that person today and connect.

50.

EVERY GIRL WANTS TO BE TREATED LIKE A PRINCESS...NO MATTER WHAT SHE TELLS YOU.

SOMETIMES GUYS ARE CONFUSED ABOUT HOW TO treat girls.

Most of the confusion comes from pop culture. If you watch music videos, it seems that all girls are sexual creatures whose main desire is to be sexy. If you listen to certain Hollywood women speak out, they will tell you that women don't need men; they can do anything a man can do. If you listen to rap, women are nothing but worthless tramps (and yet millions upon millions of girls like these rappers and buy their songs).

Then, to add to the confusion, in some circles men treat women like servants or slaves, claiming that women are supposed to submit, ignoring the fact that the Bible actually tells us to "submit to one another" (Ephesians 5:21).

So how should we treat a woman in a world with so many mixed messages?

Treat her like a princess.

Treat her with the utmost love and respect. After all, women are our partners in life and faith, and have been since the beginning.

Let's look at the very beginning—from the first chapter of the first book of the Bible:

> Then God said, "Let us make human beings in our image, to be like us. They will reign over the fish in the sea, the birds in the sky, the livestock, all the wild animals on the earth, and the small animals that scurry along the ground."
>
> So God created human beings in his own image. In the image of God he created them; male and female he created them.
>
> Then God blessed them and said, "Be fruitful and multiply. Fill the earth and govern it. Reign over the fish in the sea, the birds in the sky, and all the animals that scurry along the ground." (Genesis 1:26–28)

+ In verse 26, after God made human beings, who does the verse say will reign over all the different land and sea animals?

+ Whom does the word *they* refer to in verse 26?

+ In verse 27, who does God create in His own image?

+ Whom does the phrase *human beings* refer to?

+ In verse 28, whom does God bless?

+ Whom does the word *them* refer to?

+ Whom did God tell to rule over all the animals?

God gave both man and woman the authority to rule over the earth. Some people call this "coregency," which is just another way of saying "corulership."

The role of the woman is important.

I asked a female professor, a friend of mine who is both brilliant and an amazing believer, what she wants from men. She said, "I want someone to really listen to me and respect my opinions, to recognize and acknowledge my abilities."

Let's jump to the New Testament, written during a time and culture when women were not respected. Let's hear what Peter has to say about wives:

> *You husbands must give honor to your wives. Treat your wife with understanding as you live together. She may be weaker than you are, but she is your equal partner in God's gift of new life. Treat her as you should so your prayers will not be hindered.* (1 Peter 3:7)

I love Peter's word *weaker* here, because it doesn't mean lesser in any way. It actually is the same term that would describe fine china. Peter, this rough fisherman, is telling us to honor our wives, live with them in an understanding way, and treat them as coheirs of God's gift of life.

Men need to treat women as both corulers and coheirs. They are our *equal* partners in eternal life, and we need to treat these delicate beauties with the utmost care and respect.

What does this look like in your world?

- Do you open the door for women?
- Do you say "ma'am"?
- Do you serve women at every opportunity?
- Do you practice "ladies first"?

FINAL THOUGHTS

Chivalry is never dead. Treating a woman with respect will never go out of style.

51

GIVE ELDERLY PEOPLE TIME AND RESPECT.

AS THE BUS PULLED UP, THE PEOPLE WHO HAD BEEN waiting gathered around the door. An elderly man with snow-white hair and a cane in his hand happened to be at the front of the group. He reached for the rail as the bus door opened and slowly began to climb the stairs.

He was slow. *Extremely slow.* The whole bus could have loaded in the time it took for him to navigate the first step. People began to sigh and roll their eyes. No one said it, but they were all thinking it: *Hurry up, old man! I've got places to go.*

Sound mean?

Driving down the street last week, I pulled up behind a car with a little old lady at the wheel. It seemed like it took this woman about a minute just to stop at a stop sign and look both ways. She was scared to go when it was her turn, so she let all the other cars go before she finally ventured out into the intersection. Once she passed the stop sign, she drove about 20 mph in a 35 mph zone!

I forced myself not to drive around her.

It might be an American thing. After all, in some cultures, the elderly are treated with the utmost respect. But in America, we're impatient on the road, in lines, in elevators. . .we're impatient everywhere. *And old people are just too dang slow!*

We're making a huge mistake.

When we neglect to give elderly people time and respect, we're ignoring our past and our future.

Elderly people each have a story. Many of them carry a ton of knowledge and wisdom of the past. They are far more interesting than most history books, if we only could slow down enough to stop, sit with them, ask them questions, and take our time listening.

Our impatience with the elderly is suppressing the truth about our own future. Someday we're going to be slower, requiring more care, and we'll need others to be patient with us.

GO AHEAD, ANSWER. . .

+ Describe a time when an older person inconvenienced you.

+ How did you respond?

+ How should you have responded?

+ What are some ways we can treat older people with respect?

+ What are some ways we can give older people time?

FINAL THOUGHTS,

Give elderly people time and respect. They've been through a lot and can teach you plenty.

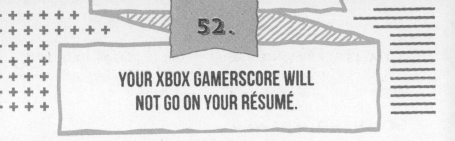

52.

YOUR XBOX GAMERSCORE WILL NOT GO ON YOUR RÉSUMÉ.

WHEN I WAS A KID, I ONCE SPENT THE NIGHT AT A friend's house and we played Atari Asteroids all night long. Seriously! Over eight hours of Asteroids. That was back in the day with a simple Atari joystick—a stick and a button. Only three commands in that game: shoot, spin, and thrust.

Eight hours of shooting, spinning, and thrusting!

Gaming can be really fun. . .*and sometimes addictive*.

Don't worry. I'm not here to tell you that gaming is evil. I like video games, and I've seen my own three teenagers enjoy them over the years. Frankly, a lot of research out there shows that games are good for the brain, developing hand/eye coordination, among other things. But like many good things, when done in excess, it can become a problem. In other words: too much gaming has consequences.

More importantly, your Xbox Gamerscore will never make it onto your résumé. So, put down that controller every once in a while and go outside!

When my son, Alec, was young, he got his first game system, Nintendo 64. It wasn't uncommon to hear Mario and Luigi jumping around in our living room or hear Donkey Kong exploring distant lands. I really enjoyed watching Alec play these games. But then I noticed something that many parents notice from their gaming kids.

Alec didn't exactly know when to quit playing.

One day I decided to test this. When he got up in the morning, he started playing games. I decided not to limit him or even say anything to him, like, "Haven't you had enough games today?" Instead, I just let him play to his heart's content.

Two hours.

Four hours.

Six hours.

Dinnertime.

We didn't even call him over for dinner. Soon he looked over and saw us all eating. "What's for dinner?"

He paused his game, came over and scarfed something down, and then went right back to his game.

This wasn't a fluke thing. On any given day, if I didn't put limits on Alec, he'd sit in front of his games all day. So we quickly learned, as parents, that video game limits were necessary.

GO AHEAD, ANSWER. . .

+ What is the longest you have ever played video games in one day?

+ What is the average amount of time you spend gaming per day or per week?

+ Do you find gaming to be addictive? Explain.

+ How can you keep gaming from controlling your life?

+ What are some of the consequences you might experience if you spend all your days indoors playing games?

FINAL THOUGHTS

I'm not going to preach to you about lack of exercise, obesity, lack of social skills, forgoing homework, and many of the other issues that arise when someone spends too much time gaming. Instead, I'll just leave you with one simple truth: your Xbox Gamerscore will *not* go on your résumé. Put your controller down every once in a while and go outside!

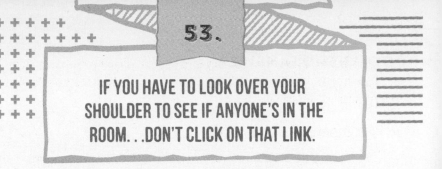

53

IF YOU HAVE TO LOOK OVER YOUR SHOULDER TO SEE IF ANYONE'S IN THE ROOM...DON'T CLICK ON THAT LINK.

IT'S HAPPENED TO MOST OF US.

We're browsing the Internet and we stumble on it, unintentionally or intentionally. In that brief moment, a million thoughts race through our minds. We know with only one small click we could see more...but we know deep inside we shouldn't click on it.

The sure giveaway was the fact that we glanced over our shoulder to make sure no one else could see the screen.

If we didn't glance, it's only because we were home alone or in a room by ourselves. But if someone *had been* home and in the room...for sure we would have checked. There's no way we would click on that link with Mom standing over our shoulder.

The temptation is real. It's on our phones, our computers, our gaming systems, and our TVs. The world offers an overflowing cornucopia of sexual imagery flowing into our homes and onto our glowing screens. Sometimes it's difficult to dodge those images.

But many guys aren't looking to dodge them. They don't stay away from these temptations, and before they know it, they're neck deep in sexually explicit material.

We've talked about this kind of temptation already (#10...also see #79), so we know God's amazing plan for sex as a part of marriage, and we know that lust can be a huge temptation we need to flee from. Paul warns us of this temptation again in his first letter to the Thessalonians:

> *God's will is for you to be holy, so stay away from all sexual sin. Then each of you will control his own body and live in holiness and honor—not in lustful passion like the pagans who do not know God and his ways.* (4:3–5)

GO AHEAD, ANSWER. . .

+ What is God's will for us?

+ What does being holy look like?

+ What does Paul tell us to stay away from?

+ What are some ways we fail to "stay away" from sexual sin on our phones, computers, and TVs?

+ How can we realistically "stay away" from sexual sin on our phones, computers, and TVs?

+ According to the verse, how do people who don't know God and His ways live their lives?

+ What are some examples of that today?

FINAL THOUGHTS

If you are tempted sexually:

- Tell a friend about your struggle and ask him to help.

- Tell a mentor about your struggle and ask him to help.

- Eliminate the temptation. If the Internet is the problem, don't go online when you're alone. If the TV's the problem, get your parents to block the channels you shouldn't watch.

- Don't even flirt with temptation. If you have to look over your shoulder to see if anyone's in the room. . .*don't click on it.*

54

YOUR RESPONSE IS YOUR RESPONSIBILITY.

"BUT HE—"

Those are the words of a fool who can't take responsibility for his own actions.

Jake and Chris are arguing, and Chris hauls off and hits Jake. Jake's coach benches him. Jake argues, "But Chris was—"

Austin is driving to school and someone cuts him off, almost hitting his car. Austin starts blaring his horn and following really close. A cop pulls him over. Austin argues, "But that guy almost hit me. I was just—"

Guess what? People are going to be jerks. It's inevitable. The question is, how are you going to respond?

Your response is your own responsibility. It doesn't matter if someone treats you like a creep, your response reflects your character.

Proverbs 15:1 offers us some really great advice:

> *A gentle answer deflects anger, but harsh words make tempers flare.*

GO AHEAD, ANSWER. . .

+ According to the verse, what deflects anger?

+ Why would a gentle answer deflect anger?

+ What makes tempers flare?

+ Why do harsh words get everyone angry?

+ Describe a time when you used harsh words. What happened?

+ Describe a time when you responded gently. What happened?

Guys love to blame someone else. If a guy gets mad, it's always the other guy's fault.

No one likes a hothead. Hotheads are always getting in fights and making enemies. A man who exhibits self-control, however, is the type of man who will lead others.

Which would you rather be?

FINAL THOUGHTS

Pray right now and ask God to change your attitude. Ask Him to make you more like Him. You're always going to encounter people who make you angry. Your response to those people is your responsibility.

55.

DON'T DO ANYTHING WITH YOUR GIRLFRIEND THAT YOU WOULDN'T DO IN FRONT OF YOUR GRANDMOTHER.

ALMOST EVERY TIME I SPEAK TO TEENAGERS ABOUT sex, whether at school assemblies or at churches, a guy approaches me afterward and asks, "If God doesn't want us to have sex, how come He makes it so impossible to stop?"

My answer is always the same: "Because you're not supposed to stop."

That always provokes the same response from the teenager: a confused look, a scratch on the head, and "Huh?"

The problem is, these guys are getting bad information. They don't understand sex, and they don't understand when to run.

First, they don't understand sex. Guys always ask questions like, "How come God doesn't want us to have sex?" or, "Why would God torture us by making something awesome like sex, and then saying, 'Don't have it'?"

If guys understood God's design for sex they wouldn't ask those questions, because God *does* want us to have sex—and he wants us to have good sex. God created the gift of sex for us to enjoy with the woman we choose to spend the rest of our lives with. This special gift was created for us to experience within the context of marriage. Unfortunately, many people don't like the idea of having only one partner.

Like it or not, unavoidable consequences surface when people have sex outside of marriage. If they understood God's plan for sex, they'd know not to get sexually involved with anyone outside of marriage, or even to lust over anyone. Sadly, many people in the world today don't want to believe that God's way is best.

These guys also don't understand when to run. You see, God created sex to be so desirable and so amazing that once people get the process started. . .*it's almost impossible to stop*! Maybe that's why the Bible uses words like "flee" and "run from" to describe how we should respond to sexual temptation (1 Corinthians 6:18 NIV; 2 Timothy 2:22).

Let me give you an example. A guy invites his girlfriend over to watch a movie with him on a Friday night. They have no intention of having sex, but they are very attracted to each other. The guy's parents say good night and go to bed, leaving the two teenagers alone in the basement watching the movie. Things get cozy, and they start making out and. . .well. . .let's just say, *things start getting even hotter*.

Back to the question I hear every time I speak about sex. "Why is it impossible to stop?"

Because you aren't supposed to stop.

Yes, believe it or not, sex begins with just snuggling and kissing. Kissing usually turns to bodily contact, then touching. . .then. . .eventually, sex.

So here's the real question young people should be asking: "How can I *avoid* getting the 'sexual process' started, because it's almost impossible to stop?"

The answer is, Don't do anything you wouldn't do in front of your grandmother.

Think about it. Grandma and the whole family are sitting there in the living room at your birthday party. Your girlfriend gives you a nice present. You thank your girlfriend and give her a hug. Maybe you even give her a quick kiss.

That sounds normal.

But what guy would start passionately kissing his girlfriend, pulling her closer, and pressing up against her. . .*in front of Grandma!!!*

Yeah, it wouldn't happen.

Why? Because that's intimate. It's meant for. . .uh. . .*marriage*.

Sex is an amazing gift that God designed for you and your wife someday. And sex is so much more than just intercourse. It begins with kissing and touching and builds with great momentum, a momentum that is not supposed to be stopped.

So don't start until you're ready to go all the way.

Until then. . .don't do anything with your girlfriend that you wouldn't do in front of your grandmother.

FINAL THOUGHTS

Those of us who have put our faith in God know His way is best. We know sex is for marriage. We know how difficult it is to resist sex once everything gets started.

The difficult part is making a conscious commitment not to put yourself in situations where you're going to be tempted to keep going. For most of us, that means:

- Don't spend time alone with a girl.
- Don't start making out with a girl.
- Don't do anything that gets the sexual process started.

Some guys pretend to be more in control than they really are. For those guys, I have a simple solution. Only make out with your girlfriend if Grandma is in the room and you are wearing a Speedo. If anything embarrassing "pops up". . .then you should probably save that situation for marriage.

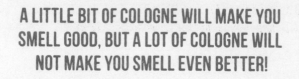

56

A LITTLE BIT OF COLOGNE WILL MAKE YOU SMELL GOOD, BUT A LOT OF COLOGNE WILL NOT MAKE YOU SMELL EVEN BETTER!

YES, SMELL IS IMPORTANT. BUT REALIZE THAT TOO much of a good thing isn't always the answer.

First things first. Cologne is applied after you shower and after you put on deodorant. If you don't do those two things. . .you're already making a huge mistake. I've already emphasized the importance of good habits like showering and brushing your teeth. I can't emphasize those truths enough. Showering and brushing your teeth are essentials. Using scents like cologne and a piece of spearmint gum are just a nice bonus, merely icing on the cake. So don't forget the cake! You can't mask the scent of sewage with a load of cologne.

But once your body is clean, a little cologne can help.

A *little* cologne!

Some guys think that spraying a whole bottle of cologne will make them even more attractive. Unfortunately, it doesn't work that way. In fact, the opposite occurs. Too much cologne can be a turnoff.

When someone wears too much cologne, it subtly communicates:

- I'm trying very hard to smell good.
- I'm desperate.
- I'm covering up something.
- I'm such a playah!

The guy who pours cologne on by the gallon makes people start sneezing.

"Wow! Who bathed in cologne?"

"I know, right? My eyes are watering. I'm dying over here!"

It doesn't even smell good; it smells like someone spilled cologne, and people will start looking for an exit.

Don't douse cologne. Just a spray or two works wonders.

Cologne should be subtle. It should be applied just enough so someone might catch a faint whiff of it when you walk by. When girls smell a freshly showered guy with a hint of cologne, their curiosity will be piqued.

"Who smells so nice? I think it's Jeff."

"I'm not sure. Jeff, is that you who smells so good?"

FINAL THOUGHTS

Don't overdo it. A little bit of cologne will make you smell good, but that doesn't mean that a lot of cologne will make you smell even better!

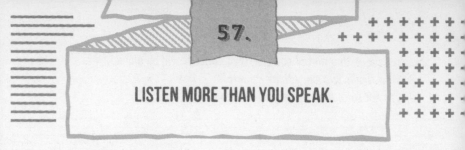

57

LISTEN MORE THAN YOU SPEAK.

IT'S CALLED THE 80/20 RULE. LISTEN 80 PERCENT OF the time; talk 20 percent.

Go ahead. Try it.

You've met people who talk too much? My friend Kristen was like that. Someone would talk; Kristen would comment. Another person would talk, and Kristen would comment again. Kristen would talk more, someone would try to comment, but Kristen would interrupt. Finally, someone else would get a chance to talk, and then Kristen would interject her opinion again.

Everyone was just waiting for someone to say, "Shut up, Kristen!"

No one likes a blabbermouth.

People love listeners.

So why do we talk so much?

Proverbs 15:2 says it as plain as can be said:

> *The tongue of the wise makes knowledge appealing, but the mouth of a fool belches out foolishness.*

GO AHEAD, ANSWER. . .

+ What does the tongue of the wise do?

+ How does a wise tongue make knowledge appealing?

+ What word does the verse use to describe the mouth that speaks foolishness?

+ Why do you think this translation chose the word "belches"?

+ What happens when we don't even stop to think, but say every thought that comes into our heads?

+ How can you be careful to speak wisdom instead of foolishness?

It's just not wise to belch out whatever we think at any moment. Try using the 80/20 rule. Listen four times more than you talk. If you're in a group of five people, this is easy. Don't let yourself talk until four other people have had their say.

For some people, *this is hard*!

But if you implement the 80/20 rule, you'll notice a few things:

- You'll begin to learn more about others.
- You'll become a better listener.
- People will perceive you as a better listener, and they'll trust you with more.
- Silence is power. People will see you as more controlled and wiser.

FINAL THOUGHTS

Listen more than you speak. This simple little practice will make you a better friend to others.

58.

YOU'RE NOT TRYING TO BECOME A BIG BOY, YOU'RE TRYING TO BECOME A MAN.

WHAT DO YOU WANT TO BE WHEN YOU GROW UP?

"A fireman."

"A policeman."

"A guy who tests video games all day."

That seems like a common question that adults ask kids. "What do you want to be when you grow up?"

Here's a wise answer: "A man."

At times, guys never grow up. Sadly, they just get bigger and older.

GO AHEAD, ANSWER. . .

+ What differences do you notice between men and boys?

+ What are some of the characteristics that men should grow out of?

+ What responsibilities do men have that boys don't?

+ What do women like about men that they don't like about boys?

+ Describe how a guy spiritually matures when he grows older.

Never forget, you're not trying to become a big boy, you're trying to become a man.

Paul offers us some really great advice in his letter to the Ephesians. In this passage, he talks about growing more mature spiritually:

> This will continue until we all come to such unity in our
> faith and knowledge of God's Son that we will be mature in
> the Lord, measuring up to the full and complete standard
> of Christ. Then we will no longer be immature like children.
> We won't be tossed and blown about by every wind of new
> teaching. We will not be influenced when people try to trick
> us with lies so clever they sound like the truth. Instead, we

will speak the truth in love, growing in every way more and
more like Christ, who is the head of his body, the church.
(Ephesians 4:13–15)

I love Paul's words here. He starts by describing how people mature when they live a life of faith in God. Think about the word *mature* for a second. How often do you hear it used in the context of growing in Christ and trusting Him more and more?

My favorite part of Paul's statement is his next sentence, when he talks about being immature like children. Look at the words he uses to describe how children are influenced by the world around us. He says, "tossed and blown about by every wind of new teaching," and "influenced when people try to trick us with lies so clever they sound like the truth."

GO AHEAD, ANSWER. . .

+ What are some of the teachings you hear at school and from friends that toss you and blow you around?

+ What are ways you are influenced when people try to trick you with "lies so clever they sound like the truth"?

Let's be honest. Most of today's music, TV, and movies tell us "lies so clever they sound like the truth." We hear messages about partying, sex, buying whatever we want; and these things always sound really appealing. The voices we hear are pretty persuasive, making lies sound like the truth.

So Paul gives us some advice in this letter about how to mature in Christ:

Throw off your old sinful nature and your former way of
life, which is corrupted by lust and deception. Instead, let
the Spirit renew your thoughts and attitudes. (Ephesians
4:22–23).

Two steps:

1. *Throw off your old sinful nature.* In other words, say to God, "Enough of these lies. I don't want to listen to them anymore." It's the first step to overcoming anything that controls us—we need to admit it's

a problem and ask for help. "God, help me to throw off this. . ." (fill in the blank: lust, anger, addiction, fear, etc.).

2. *Let the Spirit renew your thoughts and attitudes.* In other words, ask God to change the way you think. Ask Him to help you mature and begin to recognize the lies, toss them aside, and cling to the truth instead. We can't do this on our own. We need God's Holy Spirit to do it for us. Our job it simply to let Him have control.

FINAL THOUGHTS

Do you want to be a man. . .or a big boy?

Are you tired of the lies that sound like the truth? God doesn't want us to think like a child and act like a child. Throw off your old way of thinking; let the Holy Spirit renew your thoughts and attitudes.

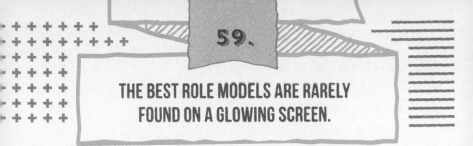

59

THE BEST ROLE MODELS ARE RARELY FOUND ON A GLOWING SCREEN.

KIDS ARE ALWAYS IN SEARCH OF A MENTOR.

They don't realize it, and they probably wouldn't even admit it. But as kids grow up, they learn how to talk and act from watching others. Their big brother, their dad, their teacher. . .these are the primary influences in their lives. . .until the entertainment media step in.

I was picked on quite a bit as a kid. Then I watched the movie *Rambo*. He was awesome! He didn't take any garbage from anyone, and he always kicked butt. I had never met anyone like that. I thought, *What if I were trained to kick butt like Rambo? Then I could make all the bullies pay!*

I wasn't much of a romantic, but I definitely liked girls. Then I watched a James Bond film. He was awesome! He always got the girls. He would kiss them, lie down on the bed, and then the scene would fade to black and the next thing I saw, he was making breakfast for a very happy girl in the morning. I had no idea what he did during the time lapse, but I wanted to do it!

I got in plenty of trouble as a kid, but I had never sneaked out of my house before. Then I saw a movie (when my parents weren't home) with Tom Cruise, in which he threw a wild party while his parents were away. He had sex with a girl, drove his dad's Porsche, and did a bunch of other crazy things. At the end of the movie, he got away with everything! I wanted to get away with everything!

Let's face it. The best role models are rarely found on the glowing screen.

The sad fact is, screens don't always tell the truth. Screens show us what we want to see. And the "eye candy" that sells big is typically sex, raunchy humor, partying, and no consequences.

These kinds of role models only slow us down on our faith journey. Consider some excellent advice from the book of Hebrews:

> *Let us strip off every weight that slows us down, especially the sin that so easily trips us up. And let us run with endurance the race God has set before us. We do this by keeping our eyes on Jesus.* (12:1–2)

+ According to the verse, what should we do with the "weight that slows us down"?

+ What are some examples of weights that slow you down?

+ How can you strip those off?

+ Whom does the verse tell us to keep our eyes on?

+ Give some examples of how can you keep your eyes on Jesus.

FINAL THOUGHTS

Movies, TV, and other glowing screens can be fun. I really enjoy them. But we need to be careful not to let entertainment become a distraction from our life of faith. If it does, we need to remember the truth from Hebrews and strip off any weight that slows us down.

If you're looking for a role model, fix your eyes on Jesus.

60

THERE'S NOTHING MORE ATTRACTIVE TO A GODLY WOMAN THAN A MAN AFTER GOD'S OWN HEART.

ASK A WOMAN TO DESCRIBE THE PERFECT MAN.

You'll hear descriptors like this: loving, caring, compassionate, forgiving, committed. But at the same time, not afraid to stand up for what is right, willing to stick up for the weak.

They probably don't even realize it, but they are describing Jesus to a T. Jesus: God in the flesh, here on earth.

Imagine if we sought to be like Him. . . .

God is the ultimate example of love. He asks us to love others above everything else. Consider Paul's words about love in 1 Corinthians:

> Love is patient and kind. Love is not jealous or boastful
> or proud or rude. It does not demand its own way. It is not
> irritable, and it keeps no record of being wronged. It does
> not rejoice about injustice but rejoices whenever the truth
> wins out. Love never gives up, never loses faith, is always
> hopeful, and endures through every circumstance. (13:4–7)

Then he wraps up all his thoughts with this statement: "Three things will last forever—faith, hope, and love—and the greatest of these is love" (v. 13).

I've heard that passage read in countless weddings. Why? Because that kind of love is inarguably the kind of love a marriage should have. If a man truly modeled that kind of love. . .he'd be the most attractive man in the world.

GO AHEAD, ANSWER. . .

+ What words would girls use to describe you?

+ What are some of the characteristics listed above that you have?

+ What are some of the characteristics listed above that you should have?

The Bible doesn't list these characteristics so that we can try to be all these things in our own strength. The truth is, we can't be these things without God. But if we seek Him with all our heart, He will slowly change our minds and attitudes to be more like Him.

FINAL THOUGHTS

How do you want people to describe you?

Seek God with all your heart. There's nothing more attractive to a woman than a man after God's own heart.

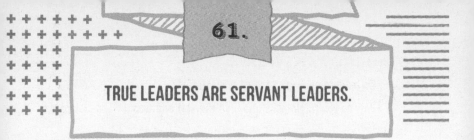

61

TRUE LEADERS ARE SERVANT LEADERS.

WANT TO BE IN THE FRONT? THEN GET IN THE BACK OF the line.

Want to lead? Then serve.

I know, it sounds a little paradoxical. But actually, it's amazing wisdom from Jesus.

Take what Jesus says in Mark 9:35, for example:

> He sat down, called the twelve disciples over to him, and said, "Whoever wants to be first must take last place and be the servant of everyone else."

GO AHEAD, ANSWER. . .

+ According to the verse, what two requirements does Jesus list if someone desires to be first?

+ What does He mean by "take last place"?

+ How can you "take last place" this week?

+ What does Jesus mean by "be the servant of everyone else"?

+ In what ways can you serve others this week?

Jesus didn't just preach it; He lived it. Consider His words in John 13:3–5:

> Jesus knew that the Father had given him authority over everything and that he had come from God and would return to God. So he got up from the table, took off his robe, wrapped a towel around his waist, and poured water into a basin. Then he began to wash the disciples' feet, drying them with the towel he had around him.

+ Do leaders and rulers typically wash feet?

+ Why do you think Jesus humbled Himself and washed His disciples' feet?

+ What kind of leadership was Jesus demonstrating?

Good leaders don't just sit on their butts and bark out orders. Effective leaders listen, care, and serve.

Think of what this would look like at home. What kind of dad will you be? The kind who orders his kids around like they are slaves, or a dad who truly cares and demonstrates it with acts of love? Will you get on your hands and knees and play with your kids? Will you help your son get ready for Little League tryouts and help your daughter with her science projects? How could you serve them better?

What kind of husband will you be? Will you make dinner for your wife, make the bed, and do a load of laundry when it's needed? How will you serve her and make her feel loved and appreciated?

What kind of boss will you be? Will you just bark orders at your employees, or will you demonstrate how to do the job and be there for them when they need you? Will you sit down with them and hear their ideas and concerns? How will you be an approachable leader?

FINAL THOUGHTS

Jesus modeled and taught a different type of leadership—servant leadership. His impact on His disciples was so great that the majority of them followed in His footsteps, serving and laying down their own lives for the church.

What legacy of leadership will you leave?

62

BE CAREFUL WHAT YOU ALLOW ON YOUR PLAYLISTS.

"I JUST LISTEN TO THE BEAT."

"It doesn't affect me."

That's what young people always tell me.

Don't worry, I'm not going to tell you that music is bad or that Lady Gaga is the devil. Instead, I'm going to ask you to be careful about what you allow to flow through your headphones.

First, let me tell you, I love music. I have quite a collection of music in my iTunes library—everything from classic rock to hip-hop. You'll find a range of artists from Bruno Mars to David Crowder coming through my headphones. My daughters and I have been sharing music for years.

Sometimes it's not easy choosing songs to download. They might sound really good musically but be really trashy lyrically. This is sad. I've had to skip out on literally hundreds of songs because they were raunchy.

I can't say I did the same when I was a teenager.

Most young people seem to think the music they listen to is "no big deal." In other words, "Who cares if I listen to songs about hooking up, drinking, or partying? They're just lyrics. I don't really pay that much attention."

Your doctor wouldn't agree.

A few years ago, a study by the Rand Corporation concluded that "teenagers whose iPods are full of music with raunchy, sexual lyrics, start having sex sooner than those who prefer other songs." The report goes on to say that "teens who said they listened to lots of music with degrading sexual messages were almost twice as likely to start having intercourse or other sexual activities within the following two years as were teens who listened to little or no sexually degrading music."[13]

GO AHEAD, ANSWER. . .

+   According to the Rand report, teenagers whose iPods are full of music with raunchy sexual lyrics are more likely to do what?

+ Why do you think teenagers would be more inclined to have sex if they listen to that kind of music?

+ Being real, what are some songs you like that have sexually explicit lyrics?

+ Why do you think most teenagers deny the effect that song lyrics have on them?

+ What kind of effect do you think lyrics have on teenagers?

+ Being real, what kind of effect might they have on you?

As Christians, we also need to consider what we are craving out of life. If we are following Jesus, hopefully we won't be trying to find fulfillment in the wrong places.

Consider these words from the book of 1 John:

> *Do not love this world nor the things it offers you, for when you love the world, you do not have the love of the Father in you. For the world offers only a craving for physical pleasure, a craving for everything we see, and pride in our achievements and possessions. These are not from the Father, but are from this world.* (2:15–16)

GO AHEAD, ANSWER. . .

+ According to the apostle John, what should we not love?

+ What are some examples of these cravings today?

+ If we love these things, what do we not have?

+ What are some examples of what the world offers?

+ Name some songs that talk about some of these cravings.

+ Where does John say these cravings come from?

We need to be careful what we put on our playlists.

FINAL THOUGHTS

Try a simple two-week experiment. Listen to whatever music you want for the first seven days. Don't force yourself to listen to something raunchy that you wouldn't normally listen to. I'm just saying, listen to what you want.

Then, during the second week, listen only to praise and worship music. That's right, see if you can go seven days without listening to any music that doesn't praise God. Don't get me wrong—I'm not saying that any music that doesn't praise God is wrong. If that were true, you couldn't sing "Row, Row, Row Your Boat." But I am suggesting that you try listening to only worship music for seven days.

After each week of this little experiment, ask yourself honestly: *How was my week?*

There's something rewarding about drawing close to God in worship. Music can help you do that.

Think carefully about what you put in your headphones. It affects you more than you know.

63.

EVERY PREMARITAL SEXUAL ACT WILL FOLLOW YOU INTO YOUR MARRIAGE BED.

WHY ARE THERE SO MANY SONGS ABOUT THE PAIN OF breaking up?

In both 2011 and 2012, Adele's album titled *21* was the top-selling album of the year. The album is basically a collection of songs about the pain of breaking up. Adele wasn't the only artist singing about heartache; in fact, in 2012 alone, almost half of the *Billboard* #1 hits were about lost love.[14]

Why do humans experience so much pain and sorrow when their relationships break apart?

The answer is readily apparent: humans crave relationships between a male and a female, and when these relationships break up, it's painful.

Let me say it another way: humans are wired to be monogamous. Guys, that means finding one woman to be your wife and sticking with her.

Scientists call this "pair bonding." Research on the subject is fascinating. In short, humans, unlike many mammals, show significant evidence of desiring to connect with one partner. Furthermore, they show signs of jealousy and anger when their partner goes outside of that relationship.

Contrast this to a cow, for example. If a farmer breeds a bull to a cow one day and then moves the bull to the neighboring field the next day, breeding it to another cow, the first cow doesn't get angry or jealous. (That's why there are no MTV reality shows for cows. Cows just don't get into the drama.)

This isn't to deny urges that men and women experience wanting to go outside the relationship. These urges are real, just like urges to overeat or to get angry. But no one can deny the consequences of infidelity or unfaithfulness of any kind, either physical or emotional. We've all seen the drama that happens when a guy cheats on his girlfriend or vice versa. It ain't pretty.

We are designed for monogamy. In other words, God made it so that a guy and girl will join together for life. This was God's plan from the beginning.

The Bible describes this in Genesis:

*This explains why a man leaves his father and mother and
is joined to his wife, and the two are united into one.* (2:24)

GO AHEAD, ANSWER. . .

+ According to the verse, what does a man do after he leaves his father and mother?

+ Instead of joining with a wife, why doesn't the man just live together with a woman until someone better looking comes along?

+ What does this verse say happens when a man is joined to his wife?

+ What does it mean that they are united as one?

+ What ramifications does this have for a guy who wants to unite with a bunch of women?

Humans are one-partner beings. When we have sex with a bunch of people, it creates problems. If a man has sex with multiple women, those women are dragged into the marriage bed.

Why? Humans are made for one partner. If a man has numerous partners and then settles down with a woman, the woman usually finds out about those ex-partners and gets jealous. Comparisons arise. Questions. Doubts. *Does he find me as attractive as his ex-girlfriend?* or *If sex was really good with her, what if he reminisces about sex with her?*

The Bible talks about the seriousness of sexual sin. Earlier we read Paul's advice to "flee" or "run" from sexual sin. But notice his words to follow:

> *No other sin so clearly affects the body as this one does.
> For sexual immorality is a sin against your own body.*
> (1 Corinthians 6:18)

Sexual sin has lasting consequences. Not just sexually transmitted diseases (STDs) and unwanted pregnancies. Sin has emotional consequences. The world would call this "drama."

Drama is a reality.

It can be avoided if we stick to God's plan.

FINAL THOUGHTS

Don't buy the world's lie. The world will tell you to test out relationships and see if they are "compatible." I assure you, premarital sex only leads to jealousy and pain. Every sexual act you commit before marriage will follow you into your marriage bed.

Save yourself for the one you're gonna spend the rest of your life with. You'll know who that is when you both say, "I do."

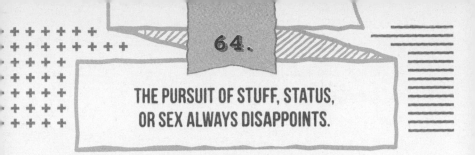

64

THE PURSUIT OF STUFF, STATUS, OR SEX ALWAYS DISAPPOINTS.

WHAT DO MOST PEOPLE WANT OUT OF LIFE?

Money, sex, and power are probably the top three choices. (Funny, I think I would have chosen cheesecake.)

People constantly pursue money, sex, or power. Think about it for a moment. Consider every gathering of celebrities. They take pictures on the red carpet. "What kind of dress is this?" They rattle off the name of the newest designer responsible for the $80,000 ensemble they're wearing. Then they go inside to give each other awards. Who is the best rapper? Who is the best actor? Who sold the most albums? Who has the most Twitter followers?

People at home sit watching.

"I wish I could afford a dress like that."

"I wish I were that famous."

"I wish that was my girlfriend!"

Let's face it. The world is all about stuff, status, and sex.

First Timothy 6:10–11 offers us some really great advice, particularly in the area of money:

> *For the love of money is the root of all kinds of evil. And some people, craving money, have wandered from the true faith and pierced themselves with many sorrows. But you, Timothy, are a man of God; so run from all these evil things. Pursue righteousness and a godly life, along with faith, love, perseverance, and gentleness.*

GO AHEAD, ANSWER. . .

+ According to the verse, what is the root of all kinds of evil?

+ Why do you think Paul said this about money?

+ Paul describes people who crave money and have wandered from the true faith. What do they pierce themselves with?

- What does he mean by that?
- What advice does Paul give Timothy?
- Why do you think he says "run"?
- How can you run from these evils?
- What does Paul say we should pursue instead?

The pursuit of money is much like the pursuit of sex and popularity. We long for something more, and we think that temporary pleasures will fulfill us.

Sadly, they don't.

That's why we see so many celebrities going through multiple relationships, using drugs, even attempting suicide.

FINAL THOUGHTS

Chase God, not money, sex, or popularity. All three of the latter will always disappoint, but God will never let you down.

65

HOW YOU TREAT YOUR MOM FORESHADOWS HOW YOU WILL TREAT YOUR WIFE.

HOW DO YOU TREAT YOUR MOM?

Do you talk to her with respect, even when you don't agree with her? Do you offer to help around the house? Do you treat her like a lady, opening doors for her and saying, "Yes, ma'am"?

Or are you a schmuck?

Don't be a schmuck. Show women the respect they deserve. The way you treat women now is a good indication of how you'll treat your wife someday.

Do you make a habit of showing women respect?

How do you treat your teachers? Do you address them respectfully, even when you think they're unfair?

How do you treat everyone, male and female?

The more we let God's Holy Spirit guide our lives, the better we'll treat all the people around us.

That's the secret that so many people miss: *the Holy Spirit.*

We see this if we look carefully at one of the most famous passages about obeying parents, near the end of the book of Ephesians:

> *Children, obey your parents because you belong to the Lord,*
> *for this is the right thing to do. "Honor your father and*
> *mother." This is the first commandment with a promise: If*
> *you honor your father and mother, "things will go well for you,*
> *and you will have a long life on the earth." (6:1–3)*

People lose the power of these words when they don't read them in context. "Reading in context" is just a fancy way of saying read the verses around these verses to see what the author has been talking about.

If you look at the verses that come before the ones about "obeying parents," you'll see that Paul gives us the secret to good relationships with everyone: "Be filled with the Holy Spirit" (5:18). Then he shows us what a Spirit-guided life looks like in *all* our relationships:

- Husbands and wives (5:21–33)
- Children with parents (6:1–3)
- Dads with kids (6:4)
- Slaves with masters (6:5–8)
- Masters with slaves (6:9)

If we just read one verse, "Children obey your parents", or "Husbands love your wives," we miss seeing how to do it. We also miss how a Spirit-guided life helps all our relationships.

How you treat your mom is a foreshadowing of how you're going to treat your wife.

Give your mom, your dad, your teachers, your siblings—everybody—the utmost love and respect.

GO AHEAD, ANSWER. . .

+ How can you specifically show your mom respect this week?

+ How can you specifically show your siblings respect this week?

+ How can you specifically show your teachers and other authority figures in your life respect this week?

+ How can you specifically show your friends respect this week?

FINAL THOUGHTS

Pray and ask God to take control of your life. Tell Him specifically, "God, I want You to help me love others today, even when they make me mad." As you encounter people throughout the day, ask God, "How would You like me to respond to this person?" Allow God's love to flow through you in all your relationships.

66

"MEAT FIRST!"

IN 2005 WILL FERRELL PLAYED THE CHARACTER OF Phil Weston, a family man turned soccer coach in the film *Kicking and Screaming*. At one point in the movie, the team goes to a butcher shop to pick up two key players for the team. The dad, a foreigner, tells the team that the kids can't go until they're done working. In broken English he proclaims, "Meat first!"

My kids and I always quote that line: "Meat first!"

Whenever my kids wanted to relax before doing homework or chores, I always said, "Meat first!" It became the code word around our house for, "Work first. Play later."

"Meat first!" is based on the concept of *delayed gratification*. The idea is simple. Get your work done first, and then you can enjoy the rewards of your labor when you're done. You are delaying the gratifying rewards until after your work is finished. Hence, delayed gratification.

Often, this is simple cause and effect. Plant a crop and enjoy eating it when it's harvested. Landscape your backyard and enjoy a BBQ on your patio. Do the work first, and then enjoy the benefit of the work.

Sometimes people want the benefit without the work. The Bible addresses these people:

> *Take a lesson from the ants, you lazybones.*
>> *Learn from their ways and become wise!*
> *Though they have no prince*
>> *or governor or ruler to make them work,*
> *they labor hard all summer,*
>> *gathering food for the winter.*
> *But you, lazybones, how long will you sleep?*
>> *When will you wake up?*
> *A little extra sleep, a little more slumber,*
>> *a little folding of the hands to rest—*
> *then poverty will pounce on you like a bandit;*
>> *scarcity will attack you like an armed robber.*

(Proverbs 6:6–11)

GO AHEAD, ANSWER. . .

+ What creature does the writer tell us to imitate?

+ Why are ants wise?

+ In what ways can people be like ants?

+ What can you personally learn from the ants?

+ What does the verse say will happen to the lazy person?

+ Why will lazy people go broke?

FINAL THOUGHTS

You've heard the wisdom before: "Pain before pleasure." "You reap what you sow." "Work hard, play hard". . .or in my house, "Meat first!"

The principle is the same. Work hard, and then enjoy the fruit of your labor.

67

REMEMBER WHO YOU ARE.

GUYS ARE MEAN.

It's a fact. Guys are not really good at encouraging each other. You don't hear guys giving each other praise in the locker room. "Wow, you look good today, Tyler."

Kids who talk like that usually get beat up.

It's sad if you think about it. It's rare to hear guys complimenting each other.

"I love the way you pass that soccer ball around the field. You've got skills!"

"You sure know how to choose an outfit. Those jeans look right!"

"Hey, you got a 3.75 on your report card. I'm proud of you."

Yeah. . .guys don't say stuff like that. Only moms do.

No wonder so many guys aren't very sure of themselves. Too bad. Because God has gifted each one of us with unique abilities and strengths. These were in God's design for us before we were even born.

We see this spelled out in Jeremiah 1:5, where God says to Jeremiah:

> *"I knew you before I formed you in your mother's womb.*
> *Before you were born I set you apart*
> *and appointed you as my prophet to the nations."*

GO AHEAD, ANSWER. . .

+ According to the verse, when did God know us?

+ What did He do with Jeremiah before he was born?

+ How does it make you feel to know that God knew us and designed us before we were even born?

+ How does that affect your confidence, knowing how much love, care, and forethought God put into your design?

FINAL THOUGHTS

You are special. You are gifted. It's too bad you don't hear it more often, because then you would probably remember who you are.

Find your gift. Discover your unique strength. God can use you.

Don't forget who made you.

ALWAYS MEET THE PARENTS. IF YOU LIKE A GIRL, GET TO KNOW HER FAMILY.

IT HAPPENS ALL THE TIME. GUY MEETS GIRL, GIRL meets guy, guy likes girl, girl likes guy. . .guy dates girl.

Then guy hangs with girl, girl hangs with guy, girl's parents ask about guy, girl avoids the subject. . .*parents wonder who this guy is that their daughter is hiding*!

It's this simple: if you like a girl, meet her parents.

It should be like this: guy meets girl, girl meets guy, guy likes girl, girl likes guy. . .*guy meets the parents*!

You don't have to become best friends with her dad and start helping him rebuild an engine in his garage, but definitely meet him.

When you meet the parents:

- Look them in the eye and have a conversation.
- Ask them questions. Then listen and ask follow-up questions.
- Show them the utmost respect, using words like "sir" and "ma'am."
- Ask for permission to take their daughter out.
- Ask what time they'd like her home. Then get her home early.
- Don't do anything with her that you wouldn't do in front of them!

I have two daughters. Take it from me. Dads don't like guys who try to slip in under the radar. If a guy won't talk with me or look me in the eye, I don't trust him and I'm not going to let him near my daughter. I might even use him for target practice.

FINAL THOUGHTS

If you have any interest in a girl, make sure you show respect to her parents.

MAKE A MEMORY.

SOMETIMES WHEN GUYS GET OLDER, THEY MAKE A "bucket list."

A bucket list is a list of fun, once-in-a-lifetime experiences or feats they would like to accomplish before they "kick the bucket."

A bucket list might look like this:

- Climb Mount Everest
- Rope cattle
- Survive in the wild for three nights
- Skydive
- Visit Paris
- Kayak the American River
- Hike the Grand Canyon

You get the idea. A bucket list is a list of memories people want to create before they die.

But why wait until you're old?

This week make yourself a bucket list of sorts. Being young, you are probably fairly far from actually "kicking the bucket," so maybe it's more a list of life experiences you want to accomplish in the next ten years.

Might as well get it started now.

Ask yourself what once-in-a-lifetime experiences you would like to accomplish. Write them down. Here are some ideas:

- Learn how to surf.
- Go backpacking with a family member for a weekend.
- Breed your pets and experience puppies, kittens, etc.
- Learn how to sail.
- Build a tree house.
- Join with your dad or another adult and live with the homeless for a night.

Now, how about some spiritual goals?

- Read through the entire Bible.
- Fast and pray for an entire day.
- Go on a media fast for a week.
- Go on a mission trip.

FINAL THOUGHTS

Maybe your list will look very different. No worries. Just make the list and show it to your parents. Make plans to accomplish one or more of these items this year!

70

NEVER STRIKE OR PHYSICALLY HARM A WOMAN OR A CHILD. STAND UP TO ANYONE WHO DOES.

"YOU NEVER HIT A GIRL."

That's what my dad said, and I knew he meant it. He always meant what he said. But I didn't have any sisters, and a girl had never really made me angry enough to hit her. . .*until fifth grade*.

Her name was Susie. She was in my class, and she was usually pretty nice. She was pretty cute, too.

But on this particular day, there was nothing cute about Susie. The ugliest words I'd ever heard were coming from her lips. . .and I didn't handle it very well.

I was captain of our kickball team in PE. I had played soccer for about six years, and I could kick a kickball farther than anyone on my team.

This was the final day of our kickball series, and our team had made it to the championships. I know, I know. It was just PE. But for our team, this was a big deal.

It was the final game, two outs, and the other team was up by two runs. We had one person on base and I was up. I had a chance to tie up the game.

"Everybody, scoot back!"

That's what they would yell when someone could kick it really far. It made me feel good when I heard them yell it. *Maybe a little too good.*

The pitcher rolled the kickball toward me, and I kicked it over the center fielder's head. (*Ha. . .didn't scoot back far enough, did ya?*) I rounded first and second, heading to third, but the center fielder was quick, fetched the ball, and threw it toward third. I beat the ball there but decided to go for it.

The whole team was yelling, "Stay!" But I was feeling pretty good, imagining what it would be like to get a home run, tying up the score. The other runner had already scored.

I rounded third and headed home.

The third baseman caught the ball, threw it home, and I was easily tagged out.

Game over. We lost by one.

The other team cheered, and my team all glared at me. No one said a word

. . .except Susie, of course.

Susie walked next to me and blasted me with insults. "You're the worst captain I've ever had. I can't believe I got put on the same team as you. I should have known you'd screw it up. Why did you go for it? You are pathetic."

I don't know what I was thinking, but I turned around and socked her in the stomach, hard! I can still remember the look on her face. Her eyes were wide, with an expression of, *I can't believe you just hit me.* She probably would have said it, but I had knocked the wind out of her and she couldn't say a word. She just dropped to the ground crying, holding her stomach.

It felt good—for about two and a half seconds.

I looked around. Everybody was shocked.

My teacher's jaw dropped to the ground. She gasped and finally said, "I can't believe you just hit a girl!"

I got sent to the principal's office and was suspended.

I should have listened to my dad.

It's this simple: it's never okay to hit a girl. Never! It doesn't matter if she insults you or calls you names like Susie did to me. Even if she smacks you. . .you don't smack her back.

Never hit someone weaker than you.

FINAL THOUGHTS

You're going to experience times when you are tempted to use physical force against someone weaker than you. Like Susie, they might say mean things, deserved or undeserved. Don't do it. Don't retaliate.

Never strike a woman, under any circumstances. Stand up to anyone who does.

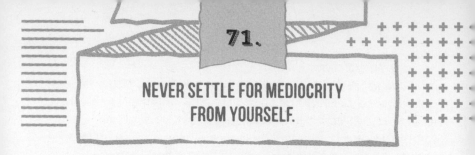

71

NEVER SETTLE FOR MEDIOCRITY FROM YOURSELF.

MY FRIEND'S SON FINISHED MOWING THE LAWN. . . *and it looked terrible!*

His son had been taught how to mow, edge, and use the blower to clean up afterward. The boy skipped out on edging altogether and never even used the blower. He just started up the mower and pushed it around the yard, leaving various strips of uncut grass in his sloppy wake.

When my friend saw his son's finished (or, arguably, unfinished) product, he shook his head in disappointment and brought his son back out to inspect his slipshod work. I love what he told his son. He just asked, "Are you proud of this job, son?"

His son looked confused. "Why would I be proud of mowing, Dad? It's just a lawn."

His dad put his arm around him and said, "If you can't do a job you're proud of, then don't even bother doing it." He went on, "People can tell a lot about you by the work you do. What do you think people would conclude about you from this lawn?"

His son kicked his feet. "I don't know. Maybe that it's sloppy."

"Is that what you want to be known for?" his dad asked. "Sloppy work?"

You might not like mowing the lawn. Life is full of chores we aren't going to like. The question is, what kind of effort do you put into your work? It doesn't matter what it is: mowing lawns, cleaning your room, schoolwork. Are you giving it your best?

Last week, when I was watching an NFL game on CBS, one of the commentators made a joke about his grades in college. He said, "You know what the athletes always say at USC? 'If you pay the fee, we'll get the C.' "

It's pretty obvious what effort these guys were willing to put into their schoolwork. What does that say about them?

Paul talks about this in his first letter to the church in Thessalonica:

Finally, dear brothers and sisters, we urge you in the name of the Lord Jesus to live in a way that pleases God, as we have taught you. You live this way already, and we encourage you to do so even more. (1 Thessalonians 4:1)

GO AHEAD, ANSWER. . .

+ What does Paul urge us to do?

+ How can we live in a way that pleases God?

+ Paul adds that the Christians in Thessalonica already live this way. So what does he ask them to do?

+ What does he mean by this?

+ Why do you think he asks them to "do so even more"?

+ Do you know what mediocrity is?

Mediocrity is doing things of moderate to low quality. It's just average. Just okay.

Don't get me wrong, I'm not urging you to try to do something impossible. If you're five foot two and not athletic, I don't expect you to get into the NBA. The issue here is *effort*, not ability. What effort do you put into your life? Are you trying, or are you just kicking back and settling for mediocrity?

Don't settle for mediocrity from yourself. Always give it your best effort.

FINAL THOUGHTS

If people looked at the effort you put into school, chores. . . *your life*, what would they say about you?

72

REPUTATIONS ARE EARNED. A GOOD REPUTATION CAN BE DESTROYED BY ONE BAD DECISION. A BAD REPUTATION CAN ONLY BE REPAIRED, OVER TIME, BY MANY GOOD CHOICES.

A GOOD REPUTATION CAN BE WRECKED BY ONE BAD choice. A bad reputation can only be repaired, over time, by many good choices. Think about that for a second.

GO AHEAD, ANSWER. . .

+ According to the statement above, what can kill a good reputation?

+ Why would one bad choice destroy a reputation?

+ Describe a situation you've seen where someone's reputation was wrecked by a single choice.

+ According to the statement above, what does it take to change a bad reputation?

+ Why does it take so many good acts to change a bad reputation?

+ Can you think of an example of someone who changed his or her reputation from bad to good? How did he or she do it?

The book of Proverbs speaks about reputation:

> *Choose a good reputation over great riches;*
> *being held in high esteem is better than silver or gold.*
> (22:1)

Don't underestimate the value of your reputation. It only takes one bad choice to destroy it.

Think of the ramifications of these single choices:

- You text while driving just once, and you accidentally kill a pedestrian.
- You sleep with your girlfriend just once, and she gets pregnant.
- You get mad at your best friend one time and you yell, "At least I'm not pathetically fat!"
- You cheat on a test, and the school makes an example out of you and suspends you.

All these are true examples. All of these irreversible events were single lapses in judgment that ended up costing the person *big-time*.

FINAL THOUGHTS

Consider each of those opening statements:

A good reputation can be destroyed by one bad decision: Our choices matter, and each choice we make—good or bad—affects our reputation.

A bad reputation can only be repaired, over time, by many good choices: The good news is, if you mess up, it's not irreversible. God's grace is big enough to cover our mistakes. And good choices put us back on the road toward a restored reputation.

Choose a good reputation. As a Christian, you are representing more than just yourself.

73.

LEARN HOW TO WORSHIP YOUR CREATOR. THE GREATEST WORSHIPPER IN THE BIBLE WAS ALSO THE GREATEST WARRIOR.

LONG BEFORE THE ROMAN EMPIRE, AND LONG BEFORE Alexander the Great, lived a man who conquered land like no one before. His name was David, and his secret was his advocate.

God helped David win.

David was a man after God's own heart (1 Samuel 16:7), and when David became king, God gave David victory over his enemies time and time again. No matter whom David fought, he won. With God's help, he was the greatest of warriors.

But God's greatest warrior was still a man after God's own heart, so he wasn't just a warrior.

He was a great worshipper as well.

We see an example of this shortly after David became king. He captured Jerusalem from the Jebusites, despite their mocking, and then conquered the Philistines (2 Samuel 5). Then he gathered thirty thousand elite troops and transported the ark of God to the City of David.

As David brought the ark up to his capital city, the people shouted, blew rams' horns, and danced. Wearing a priestly garment, David led the way, leaping and dancing and worshipping God (2 Samuel 6).

When his wife, Michal, daughter of the former king, Saul, saw David leaping and dancing in front of everyone, she was disgusted with him and confronted him, saying, "You looked shameful today, exposing yourself in those garments."

David responded, "You think that's bad? I'll do worse if I have to, to worship my Lord!" (see 2 Samuel 6:22).

I've heard many people cite this passage of scripture to defend their crazy antics, when their crazy antics were obvious ploys to draw attention to themselves. In other words, their actions were shouting, "Look at me! Look how undignified I can be." That's not what happened in David's case.

I agree, David didn't always make the right choices, but this is an instance where he was worshipping God the way a man who loves God does—unrestrained. (And if you read through the book of Psalms, you won't question David's love for God or his intentions.)

David wasn't worried about what others thought of his worship. He loved God and was willing to humble himself to express it.

Consider the following ways you can worship:

- Praise God as you listen to music that glorifies Him.
- Sing to Him, praying the words to Him.
- Give to Him. Our offerings to Him are a form of worship.
- Live a life of worship. Worship God throughout the day through all your actions, giving each moment to Him as an act of worship (Romans 12:1–2).

FINAL THOUGHTS

Learn how to worship your Creator. It's no secret that the greatest worshipper in the Bible was also the greatest warrior.

74.

PRAY FOR YOUR FUTURE WIFE TODAY.

SHE'S OUT THERE. . .*SOMEWHERE.*

Start praying for her *today*.

Think about it. If you are going to get married someday, then God already knows who that special girl will be. Maybe she's someone you already know, or maybe she lives across the country and you won't meet her for years. But just knowing and acknowledging that she is out there might change your perspective on dating.

TRY THIS. . .

+ Pray for the girl God has in store for you.

+ Pray specifically about her hopes and struggles each day.

+ Pray for her protection.

+ Pray for your attitude toward women.

+ Pray for God to mold and shape you into a man of God who will be a good husband someday.

+ Pray that your relationships with girls now will not hurt your relationship with your wife later.

+ Pray that God will help you with your sexual urges, keeping you pure until you marry the woman you will spend the rest of your life with.

Imagine if you prayed those prayers every day. Consider how your attitude toward women would change.

When we have regular conversations with God, it helps us keep a proper perspective on the life He's called us to live. Considering tomorrow helps us live better today.

FINAL THOUGHTS

What are you waiting for? Pray for your future wife right now.

75

RESPECT THE WORD NO.

IT'S HARD HEARING THE WORD NO.

> *"Mom, can I go over to Sean's house to play video games?"*
>
> *"No."*
>
> *"Mrs. Narlesky, I finished my quiz. Can I please go to the restroom?"*
>
> *"No."*
>
> *"Come on Alexis, I love you!"*
>
> *"No."*

"No" means no. End of story.

A lot of guys have trouble respecting the word *no*. Yes, the glaring example is in the case of a girlfriend telling a boy no when he is putting pressure on her sexually. I have a few things to say about this situation:

- You shouldn't be getting sexual with a girl until marriage anyway. Period. (See my advice on this subject in #3 and other entries throughout the book.)
- Even if you choose to go against God's design and get sexual with girls, if you have to use smooth talk or any "convincing" of any kind to sway a girl to be sexual, you're a jerk! And I mean that strictly as an insult.
- If a girl ever says no, that isn't something that is up for negotiation. Argue with a girl's "no" and you will get what's coming to you from any caring father. I promise it won't be pleasant.

As you can probably see from my tone (as the father of two girls), *no* isn't something to mess with. *Ever.*

FINAL THOUGHTS

Always respect the word *no*.

Respect it from your parents, your teachers, your friends, and especially from your girlfriend. No means no.

76

YOU ALWAYS HAVE A CHOICE, AND THERE'S ALWAYS A WAY OUT OF A BAD SITUATION. MAKE SURE YOU KNOW WHAT YOUR OPTIONS ARE.

"THERE WAS NOTHING I COULD DO!"

I've heard it a thousand times. A guy gets into trouble, he chooses the easy way, and then he says those words, as if there were no choice in the matter.

There's always a choice in the matter. *Always.*

Did the guy have a gun pointed at you? Did he tell you, "I'll shoot you if you don't get in that car drunk and drive home"?

Guess what?

1. First, has anyone really ever put a gun to your head and "made you" do something bad? Why do people even use this analogy in an argument? This isn't the movies. This doesn't happen. Wake up. No one is putting a gun to your head.

2. If, by chance, some gun-toting sociopath breaks into your house and tries to force you to do something that would hurt others. . .*you still have a choice!*

Make the hard choice.

Make the right choice.

Take Jesus, for example. When He was being tried before Pilate, He had multiple chances to get out of being whipped, tortured, and killed. Yes, someone basically had a gun to His head, and He still made the right choice.

Pilate asked Him what He had done and if He was indeed king of the Jews (John 18). Jesus could have easily backed out at that point and said, "Funny thing! This is all a misunderstanding. I'm not God. I'm just a carpenter. Let Me go, and I promise never to talk about God or any of this nonsense again. Hail Caesar!"

But Jesus didn't take the easy road. Jesus knew what had to be done, and He died for the truth, saving every one of us in the process. Even when He was asked one last time:

Pilate said, "So you are a king?"

Jesus responded, "You say I am a king. Actually, I was born and came into the world to testify to the truth. All who love the truth recognize that what I say is true." (John 18:37)

Jesus died for the truth.

You always have a choice. Don't just look for a way out. Instead, seek to do what is right.

If all your friends are getting ready to go somewhere and you don't think you should go. . .*don't go*. You're not stuck. Make the tough decision.

If temptation is creeping at your door and you think you're beaten. . .run! You still have a choice.

Are you ready to make the tough choice—the right choice?

FINAL THOUGHTS

Jesus demonstrated what it is to do right even when the consequence is death. Most of us haven't been in that dire a situation. For us, the cost is usually something as simple as discomfort, inconvenience, or maybe being teased.

You always have a choice. Make the right one.

77

YOUR TRUE CHARACTER IS REVEALED WHEN NO ONE ELSE IS WATCHING.

"LIVE YOUR LIFE AS IF YOU WERE BEING FILMED EVERY minute."

I'll never forget those words.

I was at a leadership retreat and the speaker was talking about our personal character. He defined character as "who we are in the dark." In other words—who we are when no one else is watching.

GO AHEAD, ANSWER. . .

For just a moment, forget what your parents see or the people at church see. . . .

+ Who are you in the gym locker room?

+ Who are you when you're hanging with your school friends?

+ Who are you in your room late at night?

+ Who are you when no one else is home?

+ Who are you when you're browsing the Internet?

+ Who are you when you're alone with your girlfriend?

The speaker at this retreat asked us, "If someone came up to you with a disc in his hand and said, 'I have some video of you, taken when you were totally unaware you were being filmed,' would you be nervous?"

Live your life as if you are *always* being filmed. That way, if someone comes up to you with a disc in his hand, you can look him in the eye and say, "So what? I know how I've lived, and I'm not worried about what is on that disc."

Our true character is revealed when no one else is around.

David writes about this in Psalm 139. I encourage you to get your Bible and read the whole psalm. David starts by telling God, "You have searched me, Lord, and you know me. You know when I sit and when I rise; you perceive my thoughts from afar" (vv. 1–2 NIV). Then he says, "Where can I go from your Spirit? Where can I flee from your presence?" (v. 7 NIV).

It's no secret, God sees us in our most private, and even our most embarrassing, moments.

Who are you in those moments?

God wants you to give Him control; not just part of you, but *total* control. That means even in the dark and behind closed doors. Even when no one else is watching.

Are you ready to give God total control?

David finishes the psalm by asking God to examine his innermost being:

> *Search me, God, and know my heart;*
> *test me and know my anxious thoughts.*
> *See if there is any offensive way in me,*
> *and lead me in the way everlasting.* (vv. 23–24 NIV)

FINAL THOUGHTS

Try praying Psalm 139 as a prayer to God right now.

Your true character is revealed in the moments when you think no one is watching.

God is watching.

Ask God to search you, to know every part of you, to test you, and to see if there is anything offensive in you. God is willing not only to forgive you for what you've done, but also to wipe the slate clean. Just ask Him. And give Him the power to "lead" you "in the way everlasting."

78

GOD SEES EVERYTHING YOU DO,
SO YOU MIGHT AS WELL GET REAL WITH HIM.

IT'S FUNNY HOW AFRAID WE CAN BE TO TELL GOD THE truth. He knows anyway, so we might as well be real with Him.

That's exactly what Jesus advises us to do.

Jesus provided a great example of how we should talk with God. He didn't just say it; He lived it. He was constantly going off alone to pray and spend time with God—so much so, that His disciples noticed and requested of Him, "Teach us how to pray."

In Luke 11 and Matthew 6, we see Jesus answer their request by teaching them how to pray. I encourage you to read both passages in their entirety. But for the sake of time, I want to highlight something Jesus said about prayer that we don't want to miss.

Take a peek at this verse in Matthew 6, where Jesus is teaching His disciples how to pray. Here are Jesus' words:

> *"When you pray, go away by yourself, shut the door behind you, and pray to your Father in private. Then your Father, who sees everything, will reward you."* (verse 6)

GO AHEAD, ANSWER. . .

+ According to the verse, where does Jesus want us to go?

+ Why do you think He wants us to get alone? (Open your Bible and look up Matthew 6:5 for a little more perspective.)

+ How can our prayers change when we pray in private?

+ How does Jesus describe God the Father in this verse?

+ Why do you think Jesus describes God as "seeing everything"?

+ How does that make you feel, knowing that God sees everything?

+ How does that motivate you to be real with Him?

Jesus was a man just like you. He understands what it is like to be human, to be tempted, to be hungry, thirsty, mocked, beaten. . .

Jesus knows our struggles. He knows our need to be real with God.

Go to God with your pain and frustration. Ask for His help with the real issues you struggle with. He wants you to get alone and get real with Him.

FINAL THOUGHTS

In this same passage, Jesus continues teaching the disciples how to pray by showing them an example. He says, "Pray like this. . . ." (Matthew 6:9). Then He demonstrates how to come to the Lord with respect, asking for the proper perspective, and remembering that we are living for eternity, not for this temporary world. In His model prayer, He urges us to ask for forgiveness, for our daily needs, and for help in resisting temptation.

Try praying a prayer like that in your own words right now.

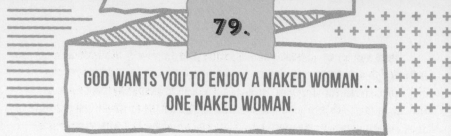

79

GOD WANTS YOU TO ENJOY A NAKED WOMAN. . . ONE NAKED WOMAN.

THE REASON A NAKED WOMAN LOOKS AMAZING IS BECAUSE God created her to look amazing. To make the most of that beauty, however, we should stick with the way God created for us to enjoy a woman.

Confused?

Don't be.

Let me say it another way. Naked isn't bad. The desire to see a woman naked is just part of the whole design of the awesome gift of sex that God created for us. But if we go beyond that design, looking for sexual pleasure *outside* of marriage, then consequences occur.

Unfortunately, most movies and TV shows don't show the consequences. They depict a distorted view of the truth. They show that sex is fun (that part is true) with anyone and everyone (that's where the lie begins).

Luckily, the Bible is really clear about what men are to enjoy and what we should avoid. It actually tells us in *explicit* detail! You might be surprised how detailed.

> *Rejoice in the wife of your youth.*
> *A loving doe, a graceful deer—*
> *may her breasts satisfy you always. . .*

That's right, God's Word tells us that when we're married, we should enjoy our wife's breasts! Bet you didn't see *that* coming!

But wait. Keep reading.

> *Why, my son, be intoxicated with another man's wife?*
> *Why embrace the bosom of a wayward woman?*
> *For your ways are in full view of the Lord,*
> *and he examines all your paths.*
> *The evil deeds of the wicked ensnare them;*
> *the cords of their sins hold them fast.*
> *For lack of discipline they will die,*
> *led astray by their own great folly.*
> (Proverbs 5:18–23 NIV)

These verses are a great warning. Some guys think, *Hey, it's natural to be attracted to a girl's breasts. So I'm going to enjoy as many of them as possible!* The Bible is clear. We can easily become "ensnared" or trapped by this desire, and that leads to all kinds of consequences listed in the verses above—none of them good. Apart from the woman you marry, don't be *intoxicated* by a woman's breasts.

It's amazing how real and relevant these verses are today. It's almost as if the writer of Proverbs knew how much guys would be drawn to look at naked women on the Internet, on late-night TV, in movies, maybe even in real life.

God has something so much better for us. Someday, when we find the right woman, we can get married and enjoy an amazing sexual relationship with her. This isn't anything dirty or naughty, and it's nothing to be embarrassed about. That's why God is so open about it in the Bible!

Don't allow yourself to become "ensnared" by the temptation to look at naked women who aren't your wife. You weren't created that way.

GO AHEAD, ANSWER. . .

+ Why do you think God's Word tells you to "rejoice in the wife of your youth"—that is, to enjoy and be satisfied by the woman you marry? (As opposed to looking around for something better.)

+ Why do you think God allows the Bible to talk so openly about sex?

+ What does God warn us about embracing? What is another way of saying that warning?

+ What are ways that guys get "ensnared" by the lure of other women's breasts today?

+ Read Matthew 5:27–28. How does this relate to what we've been talking about?

+ How can we avoid lusting?

+ According to Proverbs 5, what are the consequences if we don't take God seriously about this?

FINAL THOUGHTS

Sex isn't bad. It isn't dirty. It's an amazing gift that God wants you to enjoy with a woman someday—*after* you're married.

80

NEVER DATE SOMEONE YOU WOULDN'T MARRY.

"SHE'S HOT!"

"I know, right?"

"How long have you two been going out?"

"About six months."

"You gonna marry her someday?"

"Ha! No way."

"Huh? Then why're you dating her?"

"Because. . .she's hot!"

Funny, but this isn't so uncommon. Sometimes we date a girl for the moment, even though we realize she is someone we clearly wouldn't want to spend the rest of our lives with.

What's the point?

Why date a time bomb?

Think about it. If you know the relationship isn't going to last, then you're basically saying, "This is just temporary." That means the relationship will end. It's not a matter of *if*, it's just a matter of *when*.

The clock is ticking.

Humans are innately wired to bond with each other. The more time you spend with a girl, the closer you get. The closer you get, the tougher the breakup will be. And let's be honest, sometimes when you get really close with a girl, the temptation is to become more intimate. If you get into sexual situations with someone before marriage, a string of consequences will follow (which we have talked about several times in this book already).

So don't let the word *marriage* scare you. I'm not telling you to tell girls, "I might marry you someday." *Don't* do that. You'll scare them off. (I know from experience.) But you should only date girls whom you could *potentially* marry someday. In other words, if you already know she's not "marriage material," you shouldn't be dating her.

That means become friends first. As you grow closer with girls who are friends, you'll get to see who they are through the good and the bad. You'll soon recognize some of the characteristics you're looking for in your future wife.

GO AHEAD, ANSWER. . .

When you meet a girl and begin hanging out with her, ask yourself:

+ Does she put God first in her life?

+ Can I talk with her easily?

+ Do I enjoy her company?

+ Am I attracted to her?

+ Do we have fun just hanging out together?

FINAL THOUGHTS

The entertainment media have taught us only one thing matters: *looks*. In other words, "Is she hot?"

Hot is nice, but it's only icing on the cake. The girl you marry needs to be so much more.

Don't date someone you know you wouldn't marry.

81

NEVER FINISH A SENTENCE WITH "JUST SAYING."

I ALWAYS FIND IT INTRIGUING WHICH SLANG PHRASES catch on and which ones fade away.

For example, in the early 1990s, the term "the bomb" exploded into popularity. "The bomb" was the new phrase for anything great and amazing.

"This video game is the bomb."

"That car is the bomb."

"Your girlfriend is the bomb."

You wouldn't typically hear, "That math problem was the bomb!"

But soon "the bomb" fizzled. . .for a while. Then, after the millennium, the term came back, a little bit modified.

Just ditch the.

Now it was just "bomb."

"This place is bomb!"

"This song is bomb!"

"Those ribs were bomb!"

Phrases come and go. Another phrase arrived on the scene early in the new century, hitting with full force by 2010. The phrase was "just saying."

This little phrase is typically uttered after someone says something rather candid, perhaps even a little bit rude.

"Your dog is ugly. Just saying."

"I wouldn't be caught dead wearing that. Just saying."

"Your girlfriend is a tramp. Just saying."

How come I rarely hear, "I really appreciate you. Just saying."

Sadly, "just saying" seems to be another way of just saying, "I'm saying something I probably shouldn't say" or "I'm saying something in a way I probably shouldn't say it."

The phrase is actually pretty accurate. When people say "just saying," they are "just *saying*." They aren't thinking, or considering, or loving. . .they are "just saying."

What happened to love, kindness, and consideration of someone's feelings?

I've already talked a lot about love and the power of words in this book, so let me just share a simple proverb:

> *Kind words are like honey— sweet to the soul and healthy for the body.* (Proverbs 16:24)

GO AHEAD, ANSWER. . .

+ Why does this proverb use "honey" to describe kind words?

+ What *kind* words have you shared with someone in the last twenty-four hours?

+ What *unkind* words have you shared with someone in the last twenty-four hours?

+ How often does "just saying" come from your lips?

+ How's that working for you?

FINAL THOUGHTS

It's easy to "just say" something. We don't have to think, we don't have to consider someone else's feelings, we don't have to be loving. . .we just regurgitate words.

Try something that requires a little more effort: *say something kind.*

Kind words are like honey, and they're sweet to the people you connect with each day. Maybe you should try using them. *Just saying!*

82.

LEARN TO SAY, "TELL ME MORE."

DO YOU WANT TO KNOW HOW TO MAKE FRIENDS? DO you want to be liked?

No, this isn't a commercial, and I'm not selling you anything. I'm just unveiling a truth that many people ignore.

Here's the secret to gaining friends: *become a better listener.*

Many people like talking.

Few enjoy listening.

Many people enjoy being listened to.

Few enjoy being talked at.

Therein lies the dilemma. The world is full of talkers and short on listeners. But most people are longing for someone who will truly listen to them and understand them. If you can master the art of listening, people will come to you, trust you, and enjoy being with you.

So, learn to say, "Tell me more." Don't talk about yourself. Ask the other person questions, questions that say, *I'm interested. I want to know more.*

Check out the wisdom in this simple little proverb:

> *To answer before listening—*
> *that is folly and shame.* (Proverbs 18:13 NIV)

GO AHEAD, ANSWER. . .

+ According to the verse, what do we want to avoid doing?

+ What are we doing when we spout off answers before listening?

+ What does the verse describe this as?

+ What is *folly?*

+ What is *shame?*

+ Why do you think it's shameful to interrupt and assume we know what someone will say?

+ How can we practice being better listeners?

FINAL THOUGHTS

Don't interrupt people. Don't talk about yourself. Don't turn the conversation toward yourself.

Listen. Understand. Ask people, "Tell me more."

83.

TAKE RESPONSIBILITY FOR YOUR ACTIONS AND THE CONSEQUENCES THAT FOLLOW.

IT WASN'T THE CAR CRASH IN HIS DRIVEWAY THAT hurt him when his Cadillac Escalade plunged into a fire hydrant just outside his Isleworth home at 2:30 a.m. It wasn't the *National Enquirer* story released the same week about him cheating on his wife, Elin, that did him in. It wasn't even the discovery that he might be a sex addict who had spent the night with countless porn stars that destroyed him.

It was the *cover-up* that hurt Tiger Woods the most.

Tiger looked into the camera again and again and lied to his fans. . .and they took it personally.

Mike Lupica, in a *New York Daily News* article appropriately titled FOR TIGER WOODS, LYING OR COVERING UP INCIDENT WITH WIFE IN DRIVEWAY ISN'T WORTH IT, suggests we could all get past his mess-ups if Woods would only give us the straight story.[15] Lupica wasn't alone. Countless journalists and bloggers asserted the same. "We know you messed up, Tiger. You're not alone. We've all messed up. Just own up to it!"

Humans have a tendency to deny, minimize, cover up, and straight up lie when we get into trouble. I can think of countless times when I messed up as a kid and attempted to hide it. I eventually got into more trouble for lying than I ever would have for "not cleaning my room" or "leaving my bike out front overnight."

My son must have inherited my poor judgment, because he tried the same approach.

"Did you floss your teeth?"

"Uh. . .yes."

"Show me the floss."

Of course there was no floss. He was caught. What would have been a simple correction turned into a full-blown conspiracy cover-up, resulting in far more trouble than not brushing his teeth or not flossing could have ever evoked.

Take responsibility for your actions and any consequences that follow. It doesn't matter if it's not cleaning your room or wrecking the car. Cover-up is the issue.

GO AHEAD, ANSWER. . .

+ Describe a time when you got caught doing something wrong and didn't own up to it.

+ How did that turn out?

+ How might it have turned out differently if you would have owned up to your mistake?

+ Why do we instinctively try to worm out of trouble?

+ How can you begin practicing authenticity even in the small things?

FINAL THOUGHTS

Take responsibility for your actions and the consequences that follow. Don't deny, lie, cover up, or minimize. Own it. Confess it. The road to healing is quicker and the consequences are always less severe.

84

PROTECT GIRLS FROM BEING SEXUALIZED. WHAT THEY REALLY NEED IS LOVE, RESPECT, AND COMMITMENT.

"SHE WANTED IT."

That's what guys always say, but their perception is often skewed. Most sexually active girls give sex to get love.

Don't get me wrong, it's not that girls don't enjoy sex. But they're wired differently than guys. Guys are visual and sexually driven. When a voluptuous girl in a tiny bikini walks by, most guys have to try really hard not to initiate launch sequence—the sexual engines that begin turning in our bodies when we start craving sex. Girls don't get that way. They might think a guy with his shirt off is cute, but they don't lose their minds like a guy does when he sees a pretty girl.

Many guys don't know this. Two reasons why:

1. Guys assume that girls must think the same way we think. Ha! Not even close. They draw a much closer connection between sex and feeling loved and respected. For guys, it's more of a physical thing.

2. Guys get bad information from entertainment media. Because sex usually happens behind closed doors, the only place that young guys see women being sexual is when they're one-on-one with a girl or watching some form of entertainment media. And just look how the entertainment industry portrays women. Judging by what's on television, in music videos, or in the movies, women are all promiscuous. (Of course, so are all the guys.)

Sadly, girls watch entertainment, too, and many of them buy the lie that they need to be *more* sexual to have value. Experts call this phenomenon "sexualization," which they define as "when a person's value comes only from his or her sexual appeal or behavior, to the exclusion of other characteristics." In other words, when girls don't care if they're smart, talented, or wise. . .as long as they're perceived as *sexy*. Because the world is telling them sexy is what matters most.

Guys, we need to protect our sisters and female friends from becoming sexualized. A girl might *think* she wants to be sexual with you, but what she really wants, and *needs*, is love, respect, and commitment.

So how can we do this? How can guys who are very tempted by pretty girls not only flee sexual situations, but also help girls not feel like sex objects in the process?

TRY THIS. . .

+ Avoid being alone with girls in situations where sexual activity is an option.

+ Compliment girls for qualities other than their sexiness or appearance. "Nice job on your history presentation today" or, "That was nice of you to help Kelsey with her homework."

+ Don't watch media that sexualizes girls and fosters that mind-set.

FINAL THOUGHTS

Girls are much more than sex objects. Don't get caught up in the trend that sexualizes girls.

For those girls who believe the world's lies, show them genuine love and respect instead.

85.

LEARNING TO GET ALONG WITH YOUR SIBLINGS IS PRACTICE FOR GETTING ALONG WITH YOUR WIFE.

MY TWO DAUGHTERS ARGUE. . .TOO MUCH. I WON'T say they argue a lot, because I think they probably argue as much as sisters typically do. But the arguments seem to get more frequent when they stop caring.

And that's the problem.

Relationships take care. They require work.

When my daughters fight, I tell them, "Learn how to get along. This is good practice for your husband someday."

They always look at me skeptically and say, "Yeah, but I'm going to *choose* my husband!"

They let "I didn't choose my sister" become an excuse for mistreating her.

You might agree with their statement. Unless your parents arrange your marriage (which I hope they do *not*), then you *will* get to choose a wife someday. But that doesn't mean you two will always agree on everything. The fact is, you're going to have to work very hard on your marriage relationship. If you don't, then you might find some excuse.

"She wasn't like this when I first married her."

Newsflash: you'll always be able to find an excuse. But that's all it will be. An excuse to give up and be a quitter.

Your future marriage is far more important than that. It will be worth the effort. So get used to putting effort into your relationships.

Even with your brother or sister.

Learning to get along with your siblings is practice for getting along with your wife.

TRY THIS. . .

+   Try talking nicely to your siblings. Treat them like you'd treat your girlfriend.

+ Give them room to mess up. You mess up, too. Wouldn't it be cool if they were kind to you even when you didn't deserve it?

+ Practice serving them like Jesus modeled. Ask yourself, *What could I do nice for my sister today?*

+ Tell them you love them. Most brothers and sisters love each other. Few say it. Verbalize it. Nothing creepy; just let them know.

FINAL THOUGHTS

All this comes much easier when it comes from God's presence in our lives. Connect with God each day and ask Him, "God, let your love flow through me into others. . . even those who don't deserve it."

Don't settle for an excuse. Put effort into your relationships. The effort you put into your relationship with your siblings is great practice for your future relationship with your wife.

86.

IF YOU CAN'T AFFORD TO PAY FOR A GIRL ON A DATE, DON'T GO ON A DATE!

WHEN MY WIFE WAS IN COLLEGE, SHE DATED A GUY who was always broke. The relationship lasted barely a month.

"I wasn't looking for someone rich. I grew up in a poor family. I know poor well!" she explained. "It's just difficult to never be able to go anywhere or do anything because he wasted all his money on stupid stuff and couldn't ever afford to go out."

Girls like a man who manages his money well.

Call me old-school, but I still believe in chivalry. Guys can demonstrate how much they value a girl by how they treat her and take care of her. The simple truth is, most girls don't want to date a guy who doesn't pay. This doesn't make her a gold digger; it's just a fact that a girl likes it when a guy is hardworking and resourceful. I haven't met many girls who are attracted to a guy who spends foolishly or sits on his butt waiting for someone else to provide.

I'm not being chauvinistic when I say this: *girls like a provider.*

Understand me clearly. I'm not saying women should not work or that a woman needs for a man to make more money than she does. Not true. I know numerous couples where the woman in the relationship makes more than the man. It's not a problem.

But even in those cases, when the women got pregnant and took time off from work, it was nice when her husband stepped up to the responsibility of breadwinner.

Women appreciate a man who demonstrates his love and respect for her through his hard work and willingness to provide.

HELPFUL HINTS:

+ When you take a girl out on a date, plan to pay.

+ Bring more money than you need in case any unforeseen expenses arise.

- If she offers to pay, insist on paying. If she insists, don't cause a fight; instead, tell her she can pay next time.

- Never belittle a girl because you're paying. You're paying because you respect and value her, not because you think she's less than you.

- Dates don't have to be expensive. If you can't afford much, then let your creativity show how much you value her. Go on a picnic, a bike ride, or a hike through beautiful terrain.

FINAL THOUGHTS

If you can't afford the time, money, or effort to treat a girl right on a date, then don't go on a date!

STOP HANGING OUT WITH CHASE!

GROUNDED AGAIN?

You were hanging out with Chase, weren't you?

Okay, maybe his name isn't *Chase*. But you know exactly who I'm talking about. That guy who always seems to get you into trouble. Every time you hang out with him, you end up grounded, in detention, or in a fight with someone.

Let's face it. Chase is a nitwit.

Don't hang out with nitwits. They can wreck your life.

Think about it:

- Chase always pushes the limits.
- Chase doesn't care if he gets in trouble.
- Chase doesn't really care about your best interests.
- Chase is going to be sneaking out, getting drunk, or looking at porn this weekend, and you really don't want to be doing any of that.
- Chase is going to be working at the Quick Stop for the rest of his life, selling beef jerky and lottery tickets.

FINAL THOUGHTS

It's this simple. When you hang out with Chase, you're only two steps from making a bad decision.

Choose better friends than Chase!

88

SPEEDING DOESN'T SHOW A GUY'S MASCULINITY; IT REVEALS HIS IDIOCY.

IT HAPPENS ALL THE TIME. A GUY GETS IN HIS CAR, PUTS his foot on the gas. . .and something comes over him.

All that power!

The thrill of speed!

The cost of a wreck!

Wait. . .not that last one. We don't want to think about that, do we?

Sadly, motor vehicle crashes are the leading cause of death for teenagers in the United States. In 2010, an average of seven teenagers between the ages of sixteen and nineteen died each day of motor vehicle injuries.[16]

You might have known that. You've seen the commercials; you've heard about drinking and driving.

What about speed?

Speed is a major factor in 33 percent of fatal teen crashes.

Think about that—33 percent is a lot. That's one out of three. And if you add a bunch of friends in the car of a first-year driver, the odds of crashing go way up. Half of all fatal crashes involving sixteen-year-old drivers with three or more passengers are speed related.[17]

GO AHEAD, ANSWER. . .

+ Why do you think speed is a factor in one-third of fatal crashes?

+ What does *fatal* mean?

+ Why do you think the odds go up when more kids get in the car?

+ How do you think your driving is affected when a bunch of your friends are in the car?

+ Are you more prone to speed when friends are in the car?

The numbers are clear. Speed kills.

So why do so many drivers do it?

A survey of nearly four thousand people of driving age found that 63 percent considered speeding on residential streets "completely unacceptable" —but 47 percent had done it in the past month.[18]

Why would someone do something they know is so dangerous?

If you're reading this book, chances are you don't drive yet or you haven't driven for very long. Now is the time to start building good habits.

When you get your license (or if you already have it), you'll notice an overwhelming majority of people speeding. You'll see friends showing off by peeling out and driving really fast.

The truth is, speeding doesn't reveal a guy's masculinity; it reveals his idiocy.

Are you an idiot?

In half of the auto accidents where a teenage driver packed his buddies in the car and sped. . .half of them died.

FINAL THOUGHTS

Think twice before trying to impress your buddies with how hard you can push a pedal. Speed only does two things: it kills people, and it reveals stupidity.

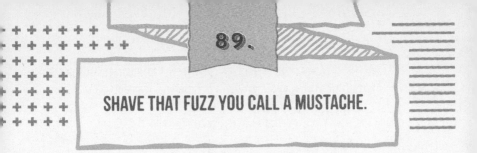

SHAVE THAT FUZZ YOU CALL A MUSTACHE.

I SEE IT ALL THE TIME. A YOUNG BOY HITS PUBERTY and he begins to grow a little bit of facial hair.

Hair is really a misnomer here. We're not talking typical beard hair. We're talking "peach fuzz." A fuzzy little caterpillar.

But what does almost every guy do? Yep. He leaves it, to try to prove he's a man. Shave the fuzz! It ain't a mustache.

Some truths to consider:

- I've never met a girl who is attracted to the fuzzy caterpillar that millions of young men mistake for a mustache. Girls don't like it.
- It reveals a guy's strong desire for real facial hair. He becomes a "mustache wannabe."
- All of a sudden, this fuzzy little adolescent can't see correctly. Everyone else in the world sees a slightly visible fuzz, but he sees a Wyatt Earp mustache.

To make matters worse, these boys usually end up stretching the truth. They'll start uttering fabrications like, "Wow, I just shaved yesterday."

Newsflash: you've never shaved in your life, but you should. Shave off that fuzz you call a mustache and you'll look far more attractive to everyone.

FINAL THOUGHTS

This book has given you numerous tips on how to be a man, and none of them involve facial hair.

Seek God, treat others right. . .*and shave that fuzz!*

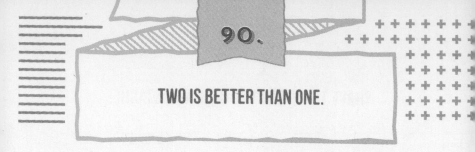

TWO IS BETTER THAN ONE.

I LOVE CYCLING.

I know, maybe it's not as popular a sport as football, basketball, or baseball, but I love it! There's something about moving fast along a road or trail with the wind whipping by.

At least, that's the hope. As a cyclist, wind can be your enemy. Wind resistance is always a factor. That's why cyclists wear tight clothes and aerodynamic helmets. They want to slip through the wind, not catch a bunch of wind like a parachute and slow down.

That's why drafting is so important in bike racing.

If you've ever seen a bike race, you've noticed large groups of cyclists riding close together, tucked neatly behind one another. They aren't just doing that so they can smell each other's sweat; they're doing it to avoid wind resistance.

I love riding with friends because we always take turns drafting off of each other. One person will lead for a minute or two, then drop back, and the next person will take the lead for a few minutes. When you're in front, it's incredibly tiring because you are enduring all the wind. Meanwhile, the riders behind you are benefiting from the windless pocket you've created.

When I ride by myself, I often average about seventeen miles per hour on a sixty-minute ride. When I ride with my friends, I average more than twenty miles per hour.

The difference is simply teamwork. When you take turns drafting with your buddies, the journey is much easier.

Such is the Christian life. When we surround ourselves with people who are plowing through similar struggles, we can help and encourage one another.

In Ecclesiastes 4:9–12, the Bible talks about the importance of surrounding ourselves with people of encouragement:

> *Two people are better off than one, for they can help each other succeed. If one person falls, the other can reach out and help. But someone who falls alone is in real trouble.*

Likewise, two people lying close together can keep each other warm. But how can one be warm alone? A person standing alone can be attacked and defeated, but two can stand back-to-back and conquer. Three are even better, for a triple-braided cord is not easily broken.

GO AHEAD, ANSWER. . .

+ What examples do these verses give of two or three being better than one?

+ When in your life has a friend been an encouragement to your faith?

+ In which area of your life could you use someone's help?

Life is full of struggles, but struggles are easier to endure when you have a friend by your side.

FINAL THOUGHTS

Which of your friends has a strong faith in God and would be an encouragement to you in your faith?

Don't forget the importance of a church family. Often, young people stop going to church when their parents don't force them to go. These teenagers who stop attending church are choosing to go on the journey of life alone.

Don't separate yourselves from the pack. Hebrews 10:25 reminds us, "Let us not neglect our meeting together, as some people do, but encourage one another." Stay connected with other believers. Surround yourself with people of encouragement.

It's no fun cycling into the wind alone.

TEN MOVIES YOU MUST SEE.

YOU'VE SEEN THE LISTS. TEN BOOKS YOU MUST READ or ten places you must visit. And they always use the word *must*.

Well, I'll jump on the bandwagon. Here's ten movies you *must* see.

1. We Bought a Zoo: Matt Damon and Scarlett Johansson star in this amazing Cameron Crowe film. *2. Signs*: This is one of M. Night Shyamalan's best films. A little scary, witty, and with amazing conversations about how to respond to tragedy. *3. Napoleon Dynamite*: Few films dive into the world of nerddom like this film. Hilarious. *4. Little Manhattan*: This is a great film to watch with a girl you like. Funny, romantic, and heartwarming. *5. Fiddler on the Roof*: This classic musical is one you have to see, a stepping-stone to conversation with musicians, older generations, and most females. *6. Mean Girls*: This film is a little edgy, but worth seeing to provide you with a very accurate insight into youth culture and the female mind. *7. Secondhand Lions*: This film is a creative combination of humor and heart, with Robert Duvall and Michael Caine. Great storytelling. *8. My Big Fat Greek Wedding*: Yes, this is commonly known as a "chick film." But secretly, you will enjoy it immensely! *9. Flipped*: Rob Reiner's brilliant story about a kid's first love. *10. Open Range*: I had to throw one Western in the mix, and this is one of my favorites. Robert Duvall and Kevin Costner show you what the good guys really look like.

FINAL THOUGHTS

This looks like a rather random list. I admit, I had to be careful which titles I selected because people's tastes vary, and different parents will have diverse guidelines of what is acceptable.

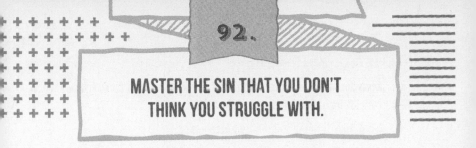

MASTER THE SIN THAT YOU DON'T THINK YOU STRUGGLE WITH.

DO YOU KNOW WHICH SIN IS THE MOST COSTLY?

I know, that's a huge question. Plenty of sins result in painful consequences. Murder, gossip, hate, uncontrolled anger. . .sexual sin has lifelong consequences. All of those sins can have agonizing costs.

One sin lies at the root of all those sins. It's the part of you that constantly whispers in your ear and tells you, "Don't worry, it's no big deal." When you're about to do something wrong, it's the part of you that says, "I've got this!," when, in actuality, you need help desperately, but this sin won't let you admit it.

The sin is *pride*. And pride truly kills.

Pride tells us we don't need God.

Pride persuades us to avoid getting help when help is what we desperately need.

If you think about it, you know it's true. Because whenever someone hits rock bottom and cries out for help, the first step to recovery is always the same: he has to admit he has a problem. And if someone is too *proud* to admit he has a problem, then he'll never get better.

Take a peek at 1 Peter 5:7 (NIV):

> *Cast all your anxiety on him because he cares for you.*

People love this verse because it sounds easy. Give your worries to God and He'll take care of you.

It's an awesome verse, but it's anything *but* easy. In fact, it's quite difficult. Probably because you really should also read the verse before it:

> *Humble yourselves, therefore, under God's mighty hand,*
> *that he may lift you up in due time.* (1 Peter 5:6 NIV)

GO AHEAD, ANSWER. . .

+ According to Peter, what is the first thing we need to do so that God may lift us up?

+ What does it mean to humble ourselves?

+ Why do we need to humble ourselves for God to catch us when we fall?

+ Why do we need to humble ourselves before we cast our worries on God?

God wants us to give Him our worries. He is willing to catch us when we fall and lift us up. He wants to take our worries away. But in order for Him to do all of that cool stuff. . .we need to first *admit we need help*. We need to humble ourselves. We need to say, "Okay God, I've tried it, and everything got messed up. I give up. I need You to take over."

For some people. . .that's where they'll stumble. Pride is what will keep them from ever getting better.

FINAL THOUGHTS

Are you willing to admit you need God's help?

The whole foundation of our relationship in Jesus is built on faith. Faith in Jesus is, in essence, saying, "God, my way doesn't work. I want to do it Your way. Please take control of my life. Forgive me for trying it my way. Make me new."

That takes great humility.

But if you can humble yourself and pray that prayer. . . God will lift you up.

TEXT MORE!

WE'VE ALREADY DISCUSSED PHONES QUITE A BIT IN this book. Probably because the phones in our pockets have become a pretty big part of our lives.

Smartphones are a handy tool. And I encourage you to use yours more. . .*for communicating with your parents.*

When I was in high school, my mom always wanted to know where I was going, who I was going to be with, and when I was going to come home. It drove me nuts!

Why does she always have to know everything!

Then I had kids of my own.

I can't even explain it. . .but I'll try. Something happens when you have your own kids. When I had my son (my firstborn), everything changed. My wife and I had joined together and created a miniature human being! When the doctors sent him home with us just a few days after he was born, I was scared to death!

What if I do something wrong?
What if I forget to feed him?

Well, we never forgot to feed him. We never forgot to get him up after his nap. God gives parents an innate sense of, "Where's my kid?" We think about our kids *all the time*!

And now that I have three teenagers, the feeling hasn't gone away. I still think about them all the time. I wonder how their day at school is going. I wonder about their friends. I hope they're safe, well fed, and happy.

And when my kids ask me if they can go hang out with their friends, I ask them the same questions my mom asked me: "Where are you going, who are you going to be hanging with, and when will you be coming home?"

TRY THIS. . .

+ Talk with your parents about your life. Tell them about your day.

+ Tell them where you're going, who you're hanging with, and when you'll be home.

+ Call them or text them when you're out with your friends. Tell them, "I just called to check in with you." They'll be shocked the first few times you do this. (They might even ask you, "What's wrong?")

+ Text your parents when you get a good grade on a test, when something fun happens, or just to say "I love you."

FINAL THOUGHTS

The effort you make to communicate with your parents will be appreciated far more than you know. . .until you have kids of your own someday.

Try it. Text your mom or dad right now just to say something nice.

94

SOAK IT IN.

HOW CAN A TEENAGE GUY STAY PURE AND NOT WANDER away from God?

It's a common question. . .and it's not a new question.

It was actually asked way back in the book of Psalms. I guess they were going through the same temptations and struggles back then.

Take a peek at Psalm 119, because it provides the plan and a simple answer:

> *How can a young person stay pure?*
> *By obeying your word.*
> *I have tried hard to find you—*
> *don't let me wander from your commands.*
> *I have hidden your word in my heart,*
> *that I might not sin against you. (verses:9–11)*

GO AHEAD, ANSWER. . .

+ According to verse 9, how can a young person stay pure?

+ How will someone know the Word enough to obey it?

+ In verse 10, what effort has the author put into finding God?

+ What are we not supposed to wander from?

+ Where can we learn God's commands?

+ In verse 11, what has the author hidden in his heart?

+ How do you hide God's Word in your heart?

One of the best ways to stay clear of the world's lies is by staying aware of the truth.

In a world where lies are flowing into every screen we own, including the ones in our pockets, we should be sure to keep the truth flowing into our minds as well. Make sure you pick up your Bible, or even grab one of those free Bible apps on your phone, and spend some time soaking in the truth of God's Word.

Yes, this takes a little bit of discipline. Relationships take work, and our relationship with God will take work. Paul made this clear to a young man named Timothy:

> *Work hard so you can present yourself to God and receive his approval. Be a good worker, one who does not need to be ashamed and who correctly explains the word of truth.*
> (2 Timothy 2:15)

How are we going to be able to live out and explain the truth if we don't know it? Spend some time soaking in the truth of God's Word.

Here are a few ideas of what this can look like:

- Find a time and a place—and make it a habit. It doesn't matter where or when. If you're an early morning person, then find a favorite spot and get alone with God for a chunk of time. If you prefer nights, soak Him in before you go to sleep.
- Use tools to make it easier. Download a Bible app. Read books that help you dive into scripture and practice it.
- Play worship music for a little bit each day. It doesn't have to be all your music, but set a time where you listen to a little Crowder or Tomlin and sing some praises to your Creator.
- Talk with a friend and/or mentor about what you're reading and learning. If you're reading through the book of Ephesians, discuss it. Dialogue about how it applies to your world.

FINAL THOUGHTS

So I ask it again: How can a young guy today keep his way pure? God's answer is clear: we need to regularly soak in His words of truth. Take a moment and pick a time and a place to connect with God and read His Word.

95

MAKE TIME FOR "GUYS' NIGHT" WITH DAD.

TIME WITH YOUR DAD IS IMPORTANT.

If your dad's not in the picture, you might be thinking, *Dude! What do you want me to do? It's not like it was my choice!*

You are completely correct. If your dad isn't in your life, it wasn't your choice or your fault. But I encourage you to find an adult mentor you can trust—a youth pastor or coach whom you can ask questions and come to for advice.

I've been a mentor like this in several boys' lives. Boys need men. (I say that, realizing this world is full of examples of creepy men who have taken advantage of boys. Just understand, that sad fact doesn't negate the need for positive male role models in the lives of young boys today.)

So, if you don't have a dad, then talk with your mom or guardian about getting a mentor. The advice I give here applies to dads, grandpas, uncles, youth pastors, coaches, and any kind of male mentor.

That's why you need to initiate time with your dad.

I speak to dads across the country and dialogue with them regularly. I rarely meet dads who don't want to spend time with their kids. Yet I frequently meet dads who want to hang out with their kids but who allow other distractions to get in the way.

Yes, sometimes dads work too much or get involved in hobbies that distract them from family time, but dads can't take all the blame. Kids often become involved in sports or other activities that drag them away from family. Dad might want to connect with his kids, but in all honesty, the kids are never there. So Dad retreats to his own activities.

Your efforts to connect with your dad can really make a difference. That means you might need to be the one to take the initiative.

Realize this might be difficult at first. If your dad has buried himself in all kinds of his own activities, he probably won't be quick to cancel softball, bowling, or Wednesday night at the church. But if you are persistent, he'll most likely make a time to connect.

+ Ask your dad if you can meet for breakfast once a week.

+ Ask him to help you with a project on a Saturday or Sunday, whenever he's off work.

+ Find an activity he likes to do and do it with him.

+ Ask him if you can have a "guys' night," just the two of you. Watch a guy movie, go out for wings and rings, go to Best Buy and look at big TVs.

FINAL THOUGHTS

When my son Alec was young, we had breakfast once a week at a restaurant down the street—just him and me. This was our special time. In addition, we would try to have guy nights where we would lie on the couch in our boxers eating unhealthy food and watching movies. (I remember him being particularly excited about watching *Godzilla* when he was nine.)

Now my brother and his boy, Aidan, have a guys' night once a week where they go out to a camper parked on their property and watch movies, just the two of them. I often hear Aidan asking my brother, "When's our next guys' night? What movie are we going to watch?"

Dad time is special time. Seek out time with Dad.

96

MAKE TIME FOR "DATE NIGHT" WITH MOM.

MY FRIEND JULIE JUST WENT ON A DATE. . .WITH HER SON.

Don't worry, it wasn't anything creepy. Julie is an amazing mom who spends time with her kids constantly. And one of the rites of passage for her son, Jeff, was "date night with Mom."

When Jeff got his license, he took his mom out on a date. She agreed to pay, but Jeff had to do all the planning.

Jeff made reservations and took his mom to a nice restaurant in the area. He opened all doors for her and even helped her to her seat before sitting down. After dinner they went and saw a movie together.

Julie reported that Jeff was a polite and gallant young man. The two of them had a great time.

Growing up with a mom and a sister, Jeff has had plenty of practice talking with girls. Maybe that's why my daughter Ashley is such good friends with him. He's one of the guys she really feels comfortable talking with.

Jeff has been learning how to talk with women his entire life!

Connecting with Mom is important. It's not weird; it's not taboo. It's actually quite the contrary. Time with our moms is an important part of growing up.

What about you? Try connecting with your mom this week in one or more of these ways:

- Sit down with your mom sometime this week and ask her about her day. Don't just ask, "How's your day?" Ask her specific questions about something she enjoys or something she likes to talk about. Listen more than you talk.
- Ask your mom if you can take her on a date sometime. Ask her where she would like to go.
- Find a regular time to connect with your mom over breakfast or coffee. Going out is fun, but if money is tight, maybe the two of you can carve out some time at the kitchen table before school in the morning.

FINAL THOUGHTS

The time you invest in time with your mom will not only help you build a solid relationship with her; it is also good practice for your marriage relationship someday.

Give it a try right now. Sit down with your mom and start a conversation.

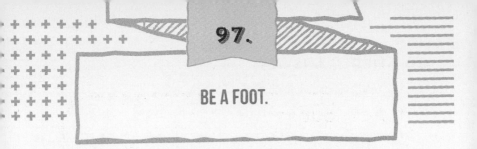

97.

BE A FOOT.

WHY DO YOU WANT TO BE A HAND WHEN YOU'RE A foot?

Depression is a growing problem among teenagers. I understand why, with nonbelievers. I can't think of anything more depressing than a life without the purpose and meaning Christ brings. But why would believers be depressed when Christ brings so much hope?

Because they forget who they are.

God doesn't make us all the same. He gives one person great athletic skills and another person math skills. (I have neither.) But we live in a world where celebrities are awarded for fame, fortune, and great athletic feats. So for plain ol' people like me, life can appear depressing. . .if we're looking from the world's perspective.

Why do we always want to be a hand when God wants us to be a really good foot?

Look at what Paul tells us:

> Yes, the body has many different parts, not just one part. If the foot says, "I am not a part of the body because I am not a hand," that does not make it any less a part of the body. And if the ear says, "I am not part of the body because I am not an eye," would that make it any less a part of the body? If the whole body were an eye, how would you hear? Or if your whole body were an ear, how would you smell anything?
>
> But our bodies have many parts, and God has put each part just where he wants it. How strange a body would be if it had only one part! (1 Corinthians 12:14–19)

GO AHEAD, ANSWER. . .

+ What point do you think Paul is trying to make?

+ How good would our bodies be with only hands and no feet?

+ How effective would a mission that feeds homeless people be with only athletic people and no one who has the gift of compassion or organizational skills?

+ In verse 18, what does Paul say God has done with each part?

+ What gifts and abilities has God given you?

+ How can you use those abilities and gifts for God's body—the church?

+ How does it make you feel to know that God is excited about you as part of His body—the church?

FINAL THOUGHTS

God has gifted you. Maybe you're not a celebrity, and maybe you don't have the same skills your friends have. God created you the way He wanted to. The question is, how are you going to use that?

Don't whine because you're not a hand. God needs feet!

98

SHUT YOUR CAKE EATER!

"I'M NOT TRYING TO BE MEAN OR ANYTHING, BUT IS IT just me, or does Dillon. . ."

Stop right there!

Someone is trash-talking.

Trash-talking. That's the word guys use, because we wouldn't even want to consider the fact that we're gossiping. Gossip is something that a bunch of old ladies do in a knitting circle. *"Did you hear what Mabel did last week?"*

Sadly, guys are prone to gossip, too. We just call it something else.

Notice. Whenever someone starts a sentence with, "I don't wanna be mean, but. . ." or "I don't hate the guy or anything, but. . ." you're about to hear gossip.

Don't even go there. Don't get caught up in the trash talk. If you hear someone heading toward this kind of conversation, get out of it immediately. And if you start wandering toward this kind of talk. . .*just shut up!* If you're not allowed to use the words *shut up*, then please just shut your cake eater!

The Bible is full of warnings about gossip. Look at Romans 1, where Paul describes people who reject God:

> *Since they thought it foolish to acknowledge God, he*
> *abandoned them to their foolish thinking and let them do*
> *things that should never be done. Their lives became full*
> *of every kind of wickedness, sin, greed, hate, envy, murder,*
> *quarreling, deception, malicious behavior, and gossip.*
> (verses 28–29)

GO AHEAD, ANSWER. . .

+ What are some of the things listed that should "never be done"?

+ Do you struggle with wickedness, murder, and malicious behavior?

+ Why do you think Paul includes gossip in this list of serious sins?

+ To be included in this list, how serious is gossip?

You'll see it again and again in the Bible. God warns His people not to get caught up in backbiting, malice, dissension, quarreling—the Bible uses all kinds of terms to describe people treating each other terribly when they don't get along. *Gossip*, *slander*—these are all just terms for trash talk. And it's easy to get caught up in trash-talking.

If someone starts to talk trash, try this:

- Say, "Actually, Dillon is my friend, so I'd rather not talk trash about him."
- Say something nice about Dillon. "Actually, Dillon rescued my cat from a tree last year, so I can't really trash-talk him. Dillon's the man!"
- Change the subject. "Is it just me, or does anyone else crave nachos right now?"
- Just walk away. Don't act like you're too good for the other guys, because you're not. Just humbly walk away.

FINAL THOUGHTS

Murder, greed, hate. . .gossip. Same diff.

Don't get caught up in talking trash. If you do. . .you might have to learn how to knit.

99.

EAT MORE COCOA PUFFS.

THIS MORNING I ATE A BOWL OF COCOA PUFFS.

That's right, I'm forty-three years old and I ate from a box of cereal with a picture of a cartoon bird on the box. And it was delicious!

Don't get me wrong, I don't eat Cocoa Puffs every day, and I don't eat junk food every meal. But occasionally, sporadically, and a little more than rarely. . . it's fun to have a treat.

If you work hard and live a life of regimen and discipline. . .every once in a while you need to just eat a bowl of Cocoa Puffs!

100.

PUPPIES AND BABIES ARE KEYS TO A WOMAN'S HEART.

HAVE YOU HAD TROUBLE GETTING GIRLS TO GIVE YOU the time of day?

Do you feel like they just don't notice you?

You just gotta use the right tools. And the two best tools are puppies and babies.

Don't believe me? Give it a try. Borrow your friend's puppy and take it on a walk to the nearest park or place where that girl you like is hanging out. Puppies are chick magnets! When girls get a glimpse of that puppy, they'll walk over and begin asking you questions about it.

Here's what you need to be ready to do:

- Know a few facts about the puppy so you can answer their questions.
- Be quick to turn the questions back to them (because girls love a guy who listens).
- Ask her, "Do you have a pet?" "What's its name?"
- Ask, "If you could have any pet, what would you have?"
- Suggest: "Bring your dog here tomorrow so I can meet him."

Puppies are a tractor beam for women.

But don't underestimate the power of a baby. Even your four-year-old little cousin named Beaufort. Bring him to the playground and push him on a swing, roll a ball with him in the grass. . .you get the idea. Girls will notice you have a sensitive, caring side, and girls LOVE a sensitive, caring side.

FINAL THOUGHTS

Maybe you don't even need a puppy or a baby. Maybe you just need to work on your sensitive, caring side or your ability to ask people questions and listen.

The more you reflect good character and care for others, the more attractive you'll be to the girl you like (*wink wink*).

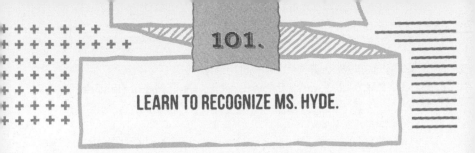

101

LEARN TO RECOGNIZE MS. HYDE.

YOU'VE HEARD OF *DR. JEKYLL AND MR. HYDE*?

In this nineteenth-century book, a man by the name of Dr. Jekyll has an alter ego who manifests himself and goes by the name of Mr. Hyde. Dr. Jekyll is good; Mr. Hyde isn't.

As you grow up, you'll notice something interesting about the female gender. It's common knowledge but not often talked about in social circles. I'll spare the formalities and just say it: *women are very emotional*! So much so, in fact, that occasionally you'll wonder what happened to that sweet, wonderful girl you were talking to just twenty-four hours ago.

Here's where a guy needs to practice wisdom beyond his years. When you see a woman make this transition, don't acknowledge it, don't verbalize it, don't even act like you recognize it.

Just flee!

Here's what it will look like: On any given day of the week you'll have a pleasant conversation with a girl (friend, girlfriend, sister, mom). The subject of her hair might come up and you'll tell her you like her hair. She'll smile, thank you, and maybe even share something personal like, "I was thinking of cutting my bangs; I'm not sure." You, being a wise young lad, tell her, "Whatever you do, it's going to look good, because you always look good."

You'll walk away from that conversation completely content. You complimented but didn't overdo it. You walked a fine line and made her smile. Success.

A day later you'll encounter the same girl and casually start a conversation with her like you have successfully the last twenty-seven days. But today something is different. You can't place it, because her beauty is preventing you from seeing what's bubbling just beneath the surface. You innocently ask, "So did you decide whether you want to cut your bangs?"

She turns to you with a scowl and snaps, "Why? . . . Does my hair look bad?"

Something's wrong. She looks on the verge of tears. Did her dog die? Did she fail a test? Something must have happened. You start to say something but can't even get in a word before she interjects again.

"Just shut it!" she says, noticeably angry.

The fact is, that wasn't the same female you talked to twenty-four hours before.

That was Ms. Hyde.

Ms. Hyde will rear her ugly head every once in a while. It's unavoidable. There's nothing we males can do about it. No words, no reasoning, no gifts can appease Ms. Hyde. The only thing to do is avoid her at all costs.

Whatever you do, don't do the following:

- Don't talk back to Ms. Hyde. You won't be able to drop any bombs on her; she will go nuclear on you.
- Don't argue. There is no persuading Ms. Hyde. Would you argue with a polar bear if you encountered one in a dark alley? (I guess this would be a dark alley in the Arctic.)
- Don't get offended. When Ms. Hyde eventually goes away, the girl you once knew and loved will return. She might even apologize.

Your best bet? . . . Just don't do a thing.

FINAL THOUGHTS

Smart men are men who know when to shut it.

When you recognize Ms. Hyde, back away slowly and look for the nearest exit.

(ENDNOTES)

1 Kelly Bothum, "Adequate Sleep Found Essential for Teen Development," *Wilmington (DE) News Journal*, August 15, 2011; http://www.dailycomet.com /article/20110815/WIRE/110819712#gsc.tab=0

2 "Annual Sleep in America Poll Exploring Connections with Communications Technology Use and Sleep," National Sleep Foundation press release, March 7, 2011; http://www.sleepfoundation.org/article/press-release/annual-sleep -america-poll-exploring-connections-communications-technology-use-and -sleep

3 "Nielsen Releases Quarterly Report on Cross-Platform Media Audience Behavior," *Press Room*, June 5, 2011; http://www.nielsen.com/us/en/ press-room/2011/q1-cross-platform-report.html.

4 *Teen People*, August 2004, 102.

5 Simon Khalaf, "Flurry Five-Year Report: It's an App World. The Web Just Lives in It," *The Flurry Blog*, April 3, 2013; http://blog.flurry.com/bid/95723/Flurry -Five-Year-Report-It-s-an-App-World-The-Web-Just-Lives-in-It.

6 Marnia Robinson and Gary Wilson, "Porn, Novelty and the Coolidge Effect," *Psychology Today*, August 8, 2011.

7 David Moye, "Savannah Nash, 16, Dies during Her First Solo Drive; Believed to Be Texting," *Huffington Post*, May 17, 2013; http://www.huffingtonpost.com /2013/05/17/savannah-nash-dies-texting_n_3294935.html.

8 *ATT Teen Driver Survey: Executive Summary*, May 2012; http://www.att.com /Common/about_us/txting_driving/att_teen_survey_executive.pdf.

9 "Generation M2: Media in the Lives of 8- to 18-Year-Olds," The Henry J. Kaiser Family Foundation, January 1, 2010; http://kff.org/other/poll-finding /report-generation-m2-media-in-the-lives.

10 "Young Adults and Teens Lead Growth among Smartphone Owners," Nielsen, September 10, 2012; http://www.nielsen.com/us/en/newswire/2012/young -adults-and-teens-lead-growth-among-smartphone-owners.html.

11 Lisa Foster, "Effectiveness of Mentor Programs: Review of the Literature from 1995 to 2000," California Research Bureau, March 2001; https://www.library.ca.gov/crb/01/04/01-004.pdf

12 Miley Cyrus, "We Can't Stop," © 2013 RCA Records/Sony Music Entertainment.

13 "Dirty Song Lyrics Can Prompt Early Teen Sex," Associated Press, August 7, 2006; http://www.nbcnews.com/id/14227775/#.Utgs4suA0cM.

14   Jonathan McKee and David R. Smith, "Losing Love Makes for Big Winners: Part I," The Source for Youth Ministries, January 4, 2013; http://www.thesource4ym.com/youthculturewindow/article.aspx?ID=237.

15   Mike Lupica, "For Tiger Woods, Lying or Covering Up Incident with Wife in Driveway Isn't Worth It," *New York Daily News*, November 29, 2009; http://www.nydailynews.com/sports/more-sports/tiger-woods-lying-covering-incident-wife-driveway-isn-worth-article-1.414000.

16   "Teen Drivers: Fact Sheet," Centers for Disease Control, October 2, 2012, http://www.cdc.gov/motorvehiclesafety/teen_drivers/teendrivers_factsheet.html.

17   Larry Copeland, "Speeding a Deadly Issue for Teen Drivers," *USA Today*, June 25, 2013; http://www.usatoday.com/story/news/nation/2013/06/25/teen-drivers-speeding/2443459.

18   Ibid.